A Checklist of
Contributions by
William Makepeace Thackeray
to Newspapers, Periodicals, Books,
and Serial Part Issues,
1828- 1864

EDGAR F. HARDEN

A Checklist of Contributions by William Makepeace Thackeray to Newspapers, Periodicals, Books, and Serial Part Issues, 1828-1864

English Literary Studies
University of Victoria
1996

ISBN 0-920604-88-9

The ELS Monograph Series is published in consultation with members of the Department by ENGLISH LITERARY STUDIES, Department of English, University of Victoria, P.O. Box 3070, Victoria, B.C., Canada, v8w 3w1.

ELS Monograph Series No. 68
© 1996 by Edgar F. Harden
The cover photograph, from near the end of Thackeray's life, is by Ernest Edwards, reproduced from an original inserted in Theodore Taylor's *Thackeray: The Humourist and the Man of Letters* (London: John Camden Hotten, 1864).

To my predecessors
in
Thackeray bibliographical scholarship

CONTENTS

PREFACE

This checklist was born out of my frustration at lacking a comprehensive and accurate listing of Thackeray's writings between 1828 and 1848 for my purposes of studying his development as a writer during those years; having compiled such a listing, I inevitably carried it forward to include the rest of his creative life. As the late Gordon N. Ray noted in a letter of 19 July 1947 to *The Times Literary Supplement*, readers of Thackeray need "a bibliography to replace the now entirely inadequate compilations of Melville and Van Duzer." Indeed, what is now eighty-five years of subsequent Thackeray scholarship requires an accurate summary. Part of our need was met by Peter L. Shillingsburg's "Census of Imprints to 1865" in his *Pegasus in Harness* (1992), pp. 242-65. The present volume attempts to supplement Shillingsburg's "Census" by listing Thackeray's other writings: those that appeared in monthly serial parts, and that were contributed to magazines, to newspapers, and to books compiled by other people during his lifetime. This checklist is intended to record his prodigious working life as expressed in these media. Immediate, authorized, serial reprintings of these writings by Harper and Brothers are included (e.g. no. 890), but piratings and printings of excerpts are ignored.

In compiling this checklist I have accepted most of George Saintsbury's attributions in the Oxford Edition of Thackeray's works, and have drawn upon the scholarship of M. H. Spielmann, James Grant Wilson, "Lewis Melville" (L. S. Benjamin), H. S. Van Duzer, Harold S. Gulliver, Gordon N. Ray, Edward M. White, Donald Hawes, and others, profiting from their appropriate scepticism as well as from their discoveries. In cases where Thackeray's authorship is not well known, I include brief parenthetical citations of authority. Checklist entries appearing within brackets represent probable, not positive attributions. Early Thackerayan contributions, like those to *The National Standard*, are no doubt under-represented, but that seems inevitable, given the lack of sufficiently persuasive evidence in individual cases.

Besides listing Thackeray's serial writings and his prose and poetic contributions to various publications, I also include the illustrations by Thackeray that accompany them, as well as Thackeray's signed *Punch* illustrations for the work of other writers—his "signature" being a pair of spectacles with crossed temples. The unsigned drawings accompanying Thackeray's own contributions to *Punch*, however, present special difficulties, since they require notice but often cannot positively be attributed to him. Therefore, when these accompanying drawings are described simply, for example, as "two illustrations," the reader should understand that their attribution is uncertain, though in the case of the mostly unsigned illustrations for works like *The Snobs of England*, the probability of his authorship is high. Illustrations accompanying Thackeray's writings that were probably not drawn by him, or that were definitely drawn by another artist, appear within brackets. Unsigned illustrations accompanying the works of other writers in *Punch*, and reprinted as works of Thackeray in Volume 9 of the Oxford Edition because of their identification by W. Lawrence Bradbury, appear here in an appendix, since the basis for that identification is unknown.

Until now the chief bibliographical source has been Benjamin's compilation of 1910 (see Abbreviations). My checklist excludes 65 of his entries for lack of sufficiently persuasive supporting evidence. On the other hand, this checklist, drawing upon the discoveries of Thackeray scholarship during the intervening eighty-five years, adds 114 new entries, which constitute 11 per cent of the total of 1033. After consulting the original Thackeray works, I have corrected the titles and dates of a number of entries listed in Benjamin, and have supplied missing page numbers for them, as well as indications of whether or not the illustrations are signed. I have identified 77 of these attributions as probable (almost all of them early works) and 957 as certain.

For assistance in preparing this checklist I am indebted to the staff of the interlibrary loans division of Simon Fraser University; to librarians at Princeton University Library, the Pierpont Morgan Library, the Berg Collection, The New York Public Library, Astor, Lenox, and Tilden Foundations, Yale University Library, the Houghton Library, Harvard University, the Boston Public Library, and the British Library; to Henry Summerfield for helpful suggestions and corrections; to Anita Mahoney of the Dean of Arts office, Simon Fraser University; and to a grant from the Social Sciences and Humanities Research Council of Canada.

ABBREVIATIONS

Adversity   Gordon N. Ray. *Thackeray: The Uses of Adversity*. New York: McGraw-Hill, 1955.

Benjamin   "Lewis Melville" [L. S. Benjamin]. *William Makepeace Thackeray*. 2 vols. London: John Lane, 1910, 2: 149-376.

"Chronicle"   *William Makepeace Thackeray: Contributions to the "Morning Chronicle."* Ed. Gordon N. Ray. Urbana: University of Illinois Press, 1955.

Cole   Sir Henry Cole. *Fifty Years of Public Work*. 2 vols. London: George Bell, 1884.

Guivarc'h   Jean Guivarc'h. "Deux journalistes anglais de Paris en 1835 (George W. M. Reynolds et W. M. T.)." *Études Anglaises*, 28 (1975): 203-12.

Gulliver   Harold S. Gulliver. *Thackeray's Literary Apprenticeship*. Valdosto, Ga.: privately printed, 1934.

Letters   *The Letters and Private Papers of William Makepeace Thackeray*. Ed. Gordon N. Ray. 4 vols. Cambridge, Mass.: Harvard University Press, 1945-46.

Letters [H]   *The Letters and Private Papers of William Makepeace Thackeray*. Ed. Edgar F. Harden. 2 vols. New York: Garland, 1994.

Miscellanies   William Makepeace Thackeray. *Miscellanies*. 4 vols. London: Bradbury and Evans, 1855-57.

"Punch"   Gordon N. Ray. "Thackeray and 'Punch': 44 Newly Identified Contributions." *The Times Literary Supplement*, 1 Jan. 1949, p. 16.

Spielmann   M. H. Spielmann. *The Hitherto Unidentified Contributions of W. M. Thackeray to "Punch."* New York: Harper & Brothers, 1900.

Stokes   Geoffrey C. Stokes. "Thackeray as Historian: Two
                  Newly Identified Contributions to *Fraser's Magazine.*"
                  Nineteenth-Century Fiction, 22 (1967-68): 281-88.

Summerfield   Henry Summerfield. "Six Newly Discovered Articles by
                  Thackeray." *Journal of the Maharaja Sayajirao University
                  of Baroda,* 12 (1963): 43-51; reprinted as *"Letters
                  from a Club Arm-Chair*: William Makepeace Thackeray."
                  Nineteenth-Century Fiction, 18 (1963-64): 205-33.

Wellesley   *The Wellesley Index to Victorian Periodicals 1824-1900.* Ed.
                  Walter E. Houghton, et al. 5 vols. Toronto: University of
                  Toronto Press, 1966-89.

White   Edward M. White. "Thackeray's Contributions to *Fraser's
                  Magazine.*" *Studies in Bibliography,* 19 (1966): 67-84.

Works   *The Oxford Thackeray.* 17 vols. London: Oxford Univer-
                  sity Press, 1908.

1828

1. "Irish Melody. (Air: 'The Minstrel Boy')." *Flindell's Western Luminary and Family Newspaper*, 4 Nov., p. 5. (Gulliver, pp. 1-2)

2. ["The Tear." Signed "T." *Flindell's Western Luminary and Family Newspaper*, 25 Nov., p. 6.] (Gulliver, pp. 5-6)

3. ["A Translation of the First Ode of Anacreon." Signed "W. M. T." *Flindell's Western Luminary and Family Newspaper*, 9 Dec., p. 6.] (Gulliver, pp. 5-6)

1829

4. "Timbuctoo." Signed "T." With an illustration. *The Snob*, 30 Apr., pp. 18-21.

5. "To Genevieve. A Disinterested Epistle." Signed "A Literary Snob." *The Snob*, 14 May, p. 31. (*Letters*, 1: 77)

6. "Advertisement." *The Snob*, 14 May, p. 34. (*Letters*, 1: 77)

7. ["Mrs. Ramsbottom in Cambridge." Signed "Dorothea Julia Ramsbottom." *The Snob*, 21 May, pp. 39-40.]

8. "The Blood-Stained Murderer; or, the Cock and the Charley." [Written with William Williams.] *The Snob*, 28 May, pp. 41-46. (*Letters*, 1: 79)

9. ["A Statement of Fax Relative to the Late Murder. By D. J. Ramsbottom." *The Snob*, 4 June, pp. 47-48.]

10. ["To the Free and Independent Snobs of Cambridge!" Signed "D. J. Ramsbottom." *The Snob*, 11 June, p. 53.]

11. ["Letter from Mrs. Ramsbottom." Signed "Dorothea Julia R——." *The Gownsman*, 12 Nov., pp. 10-12.]

12. "Modern Songs. No. 5—'I'd be a Tadpole.' Air: 'I'd be a Butterfly.'" Signed "Ø." *The Gownsman*, 12 Nov., pp. 14-15. (Gulliver, p. 18)

1830

13. "From Anacreon." Signed "Ø." *The Gownsman*, 3 Dec., p. 39. (Gulliver, p. 19)

14. ["Dedication" (to the bound volume). *The Gownsman*, p. (iii).]

1831

15. "The Stars." *Chaos*, 2 (ca. 27 Oct.): 40. (Gulliver, p. 31)

1833

16. "Louis Philippe." With an illustration. *The National Standard*, 1 (4 May): 273.   (*Letters*, 1: 259-60)

17. ["Drama. King's Theatre." *The National Standard*, 1 (4 May): 286-87.]   (Gulliver, p. 41)

18. "Address." *The National Standard*, 1 (11 May): 289.

19. ["Mr. Braham. Sonnet.—By W. Wordsworth." With an illustration. *The National Standard*, 1 (11 May): 289.]

20. ["N. M. Rothschild, Esq." With an illustration. *The National Standard*, 1 (18 May): 305.]

21. ["(London Characters. No. 1.)" With an illustration. *The National Standard*, 1 (25 May): 321.]

22. ["A. Bunn." With an illustration. *The National Standard*, 1 (1 June): 345.]

23. ["Love in Fetters. A Tottenham-Court-Road Ditty." With an illustration. *The National Standard*, 1 (8 June): 362.]

24. ["*Woman: The Angel of Life. A Poem.* By Robert Montgomery." *The National Standard*, 1 (15 June): 376-77.]

25. ["Drama. Covent Garden." Signed "Gamma." With an illustration. *The National Standard*, 1 (15 June): 380-81.]

26. ["Foreign Correspondence." With an illustration. *The National Standard*, 1 (29 June): 412-13.]

27. ["Foreign Correspondence." With an illustration. *The National Standard*, 2 (6 July): 10-11.]

28. ["Foreign Correspondence. The Charruas." With an illustration. *The National Standard*, 2 (13 July): 28-29.]

29. ["Foreign Correspondence." With an illustration. *The National Standard*, 2 (20 July): 42-43.]

30. "The Devil's Wager." With an illustration. *The National Standard*, 2 (10 Aug.): 85-86.   (*Paris Sketch Book*)

31. "The Devil's Wager." *The National Standard*, 2 (24 Aug.): 121-22.

32. "Original Papers. A Tale of Wonder." *The National Standard*, 2 (12 Oct.): 228-29.   (*Letters*, 1: 268)

33. ["Our Leader." *The National Standard*, 2 (30 Nov.): 333.]

34. ["Address." *The National Standard*, 2 (28 Dec.): 397.]

1834

35. ["Father Gahagan's Exhortation." *The National Standard*, 3 (18 Jan.): 44.]

36. "Drama. Plays and Play-Bills." Signed "Ø." *The National Standard*, 3 (25 Jan.): 62.

37. "Original Papers. *Étude sur Mirabeau*. Par Victor Hugo." Signed "Ø." *The National Standard*, 3 (1 Feb.): 75-76.

38. "The Fraser Papers for May. 'Il était un Roi d'Yvetot—Béranger.'" *Fraser's Magazine*, 9 (May): 617-18.   (*Paris Sketch Book*)

1835

39. ["La vérité sur les Cent Jours, par L. Bonaparte, Prince de Canino, Paris, 1835." Signed "W. M. T." *The Paris Literary Gazette*, 27 Oct., pp. 3-5.]   (Guivarc'h, p. 205)

40. ["Souvenirs d'Antony, par A. Dumas, Paris, Dumont, 1835." Signed "W. M. T." *The Paris Literary Gazette*, 3 Nov., pp. 19-21.]
                    (Guivarc'h, p. 205)

41. ["England." Signed "W. M. T." *The Paris Literary Gazette*, 10 Nov., pp. 33-34.]   (Guivarc'h, p. 205)

42. ["Servitude et Grandeur Militaires, par le Comte A. de Vigny, Paris, 1835." Signed "W. M. T." *The Paris Literary Gazette*, 24 Nov., pp. 65-67.]   (Guivarc'h, p. 205)

43. ["German Songs." Signed "W. M. T." *The Paris Literary Gazette*, 29 Dec., pp. 145-47.]   (Guivarc'h, p. 205)

1836

44. "(From a Private Correspondent.) Paris, Sept. 17." Signed "T. T." *The Constitutional*, 19 Sept., p. [2].   (*Letters*, 1: 324)

45. "From Our Own Correspondent. Paris, Sept. 22." Signed T. T." *The Constitutional*, 24 Sept., p. [3].

46. "Paris. From Our Own Correspondent. By Express. Paris, Sept. 25." Signed "T. T." *The Constitutional*, 27 Sept., p. [3].

47. "Paris. From Our Own Correspondent. By Express." Signed "T. T." *The Constitutional*, 29 Sept., p. [3].

48. "(From Our Own Correspondent.) Paris, Sept. 28." Signed "T. T." *The Constitutional*, 1 Oct., p. [2].

80. "Paris. From Our Own Correspondent. On Some New State Maxims in France. Jan. 9." Signed "T. T." *The Constitutional*, 13 Jan., p. [3].

81. "Paris. From Our Own Correspondent. The Addresses of the Chambers.—Marshal Soult on the Art. of War.—The Strasburg Conspiracy. Jan. 11." Signed "T. T." *The Constitutional*, 14 Jan., p. [3].

82. "Paris. From Our Own Correspondent. The Chamber of Deputies. —The Occult Power.—The Motion of M. Barrot.—The Latest Fashionable Intelligence." Signed "T. T." *The Constitutional*, 18 Jan., p. [3].

83. "Paris. From Our Own Correspondent. The Last Defeat of the Carlists.—The Spy System in Switzerland and at Strasburg. Jan. 16." Signed "T. T." *The Constitutional*, 19 Jan., p. [3].

84. "Paris. From Our Own Correspondent. M. Guizot's Recantation— Berryer and Thiers—The Choice of Dupin. Jan. 18." Signed "T. T." *The Constitutional*, 21 Jan., p. [3].

85. "Paris. (From Our Own Correspondent.) The Victory of the Ministry—The Strasburg Verdict. Jan. 21." Signed "T. T." *The Constitutional*, 24 Jan., p. [3].

86. "Paris. (From Our Own Correspondent.) Some New Laws of Repression.—A New French Siberia.—Ministerial Quarrels. Jan. 25." Signed "T. T." *The Constitutional*, 28 Jan., p. [3].

87. "Paris. From Our Own Correspondent. Jan. 28." Signed "T. T." *The Constitutional*, 31 Jan., p. [3].

88. "Foreign Correspondence. Paris, January 31. (From Our Own Correspondent.)" Signed "T. T." *The Constitutional*, 3 Feb., p. [4].

89. "Foreign Correspondence. Paris, February 5. (From Our Own Correspondent.)" Signed "T. T." *The Constitutional*, 8 Feb., p. [4].

90. "Foreign Correspondence. Paris. February 8. (From Our Own Correspondent.)" Signed "T. T." *The Constitutional*, 11 Feb., p. [3].

91. "Foreign Correspondence. (From Our Own Correspondent.) Paris, Feb. 15. Spanish Affairs—M. Dupin's Explanations—M. Clausel's Recal. M. Salvandy's Patriotism." Signed "T. T." *The Constitutional*, 18 Feb., p. [3].

92. ["To the Readers of the Constitutional." *The Constitutional*, 1 July, p. (3).]

93. "The French Revolution, by T. Carlyle." *The Times*, 3 Aug., p. 6.

94. "The Professor.—A Tale. By Goliah Gahagan." *Bentley's Miscellany*, 2 (Sept.): 277-88.

95. "The Yellowplush Correspondence. [No. I.] Fashnable Fax and Polite Annygoats. By Charles Yellowplush, Esq." *Fraser's Magazine*, 16 (Nov.): 644-49.

96. ["A Word on the Annuals." *Fraser's Magazine*, 16 (Dec.): 757-63.]
(White, p. 79)

97. [Three illustrations to John Barrow. *King Glumpus: An Interlude in One Act.* (For private circulation only.) London: privately printed, 1837.]

1838

98. "The Yellowplush Correspondence. No. II. Miss Shum's Husband." With an illustration. *Fraser's Magazine*, 17 (Jan.): 39-49.

99. "Our Batch of Novels for Christmas, 1837." *Fraser's Magazine*, 17 (Jan.): 79-92. (*Letters*, 1: 514)

100. "Duchess of Marlborough's Private Correspondence." *The Times*, 6 Jan., p. 6. (*Letters*, 1: 515)

101. "Eros and Anteros—or 'Love,' by Lady Charlotte Bury" and "A Diary Relative to George IV. and Queen Caroline." *The Times*, 11 Jan., p. 3. (*Letters*, 1: 515)

102. "Memoirs of Holt, The Irish Rebel." *The Times*, 31 Jan., p. 2. (*Letters*, 1: 515)

103. "The Yellowplush Correspondence. No. III. Dimond Cut Dimond." With an illustration. *Fraser's Magazine*, 17 (Feb.): 243-50.

104. "Some Passages in the Life of Major Gahagan." *The New Monthly Magazine*, 52 (Feb.): 174-82.

105. "Half-a-Crown's Worth of Cheap Knowledge." *Fraser's Magazine*, 17 (Mar.): 279-90. (*Letters*, 1: 515)

106. "The Yellowplush Correspondence. No. IV. Skimmings from 'The Dairy of George IV.'" *Fraser's Magazine*, 17 (Mar.): 353-59.

107. "Historical Recollections by Major Gahagan." *The New Monthly Magazine*, 52 (Mar.): 374-78.

108. "The Yellowplush Correspondence. No. V. Foring Parts." With an illustration. *Fraser's Magazine*, 17 (Apr.): 404-08.

109. "The Exhibition at Paris." Signed "D. D." *The Times*, 5 Apr., p. 5.
(*Letters*, 1: 361)

110. "The Poetical Works of Dr. Southey, Collected by Himself." *The Times*, 17 Apr., p. 6.
(*Letters*, 1: 516)

111. "Four German Ditties." *Fraser's Magazine*, 17 (May): 577-79.
(*Miscellanies*)

112. "The Yellowplush Correspondence. No. VI. Mr. Deuceace at Paris [Chaps. I-IV]." With an illustration. *Fraser's Magazine*, 17 (May): 616-27.

113. ["Mr. Carlyle's Lectures." *The Times*, 1 May, p. 5.]

114. "The Yellowplush Correspondence. Mr. Deuceace at Paris. No. II [Chaps. V-VII]." *Fraser's Magazine*, 17 (June): 734-41.

115. "Strictures on Pictures. A Letter from Michael Angelo Titmarsh, Esq." *Fraser's Magazine*, 17 (June): 758-64.

116. "The Yellowplush Correspondence. The End of Mr. Deuceace's History [Chaps. VIII-X]." With an illustration. *Fraser's Magazine*, 18 (July): 59-71.

117. "The Yellowplush Correspondence. Mr. Yellowplush's Ajew." *Fraser's Magazine*, 18 (Aug.): 195-200.

118. "City of the Czar." *The Times*, 30 Aug., p. 3.   (*Letters [H]*, 1: 38)

119. "The City of the Czar." *The Times*, 7 Sept., p. 2. (*Letters [H]*, 1: 38)

120. "The Story of Mary Ancel." *The New Monthly Magazine*, 54 (Oct.): 185-97.
(*Paris Sketch Book*)

121. "Major Gahagan's Historical Reminiscences." *The New Monthly Magazine*, 54 (Nov. 1838): 319-28.

122. "The Annuals." *The Times*, 2 Nov., p. 5.   (*Letters*, 1: 375)

123. "Steam Navigation in the Pacific." *The Times*, 8 Nov., p. 5.
(*Letters*, 1: 375)

124. "Tyler's Life of Henry V." *The Times*, 12 Nov., pp. 2-3. (*Letters*, 1: 375)

125. "Fraser's Winter Journey to Persia." *The Times*, 16 Nov.; p. 3.
(*Letters*, 1: 375)

126. "Count Valerian Krasinski's History of the Reformation in Poland." *The Times*, 27 Nov., p. 3.   (*Letters*, 1: 375)

127. "The Painter's Bargain. Communicated by Michael Angelo Titmarsh, Esq." *Fraser's Magazine*, 18 (Dec.): 687-93. (*Paris Sketch Book*)

128. "Major Gahagan's Historical Reminiscences." *The New Monthly Magazine*, 54 (Dec.): 543-52.

129. Twelve illustrations to Douglas Jerrold, *Men of Character*. 3 vols. London: Henry Colburn, 1838.

130. Ten [in some copies eighteen] illustrations to Charles G. Addison. *Damascus and Palmyra*. 2 vols. London: Richard Bentley, 1838.
(*Letters*, 1: 513)

131. "Stubbs's Calendar; or, The Fatal Boots." *The Comic Almanack for 1839, With Twelve Illustrations of the Months, by Geo. Cruikshank.* London: Charles Tilt, [1838], pp. 4-5, 8-9, 12-13, 16-17, 20-21, 24-25, 28-29, 32-33, 36-37, 40-41, 44-45, 48-49.

1839

132. "Our Annual Execution." *Fraser's Magazine*, 19 (Jan.): 57-67.
(*Miscellanies*)

133. ["Manners and Society in St. Petersburg." *The British and Foreign Review*, 8 (Jan.): 33-63.] (*Letters [H]*, 1: 38)

134. "Major Gahagan's Historical Reminiscences." *The New Monthly Magazine*, 55 (Feb.): 266-81.

135. ["Le Duc de Normandie," *Fraser's Magazine*, 19 (Feb.): 192-204.]
(Stokes, p. 285)

136. ["Horæ Catnachianæ." *Fraser's Magazine*, 19 (Apr.): 407-24.]
(White, p. 80)

137. "Speeches of Lord Brougham." *The British and Foreign Review*, 8 (Apr.): 490-539. (*Letters*, 1: 388)

138. "Parisian Caricatures." Signed "T." *The London and Westminster Review*, 32 (Apr.): 282-305. (*Paris Sketch Book*)

139. "Catherine: A Story [Chap. I]. By Ikey Solomons, Esq. Junior." With an illustration. *Fraser's Magazine*, 19 (May): 604-17.

140. "Catherine : A Story [Chaps. II-IV]. By Ikey Solomons, Esq. Junior." With an illustration. *Fraser's Magazine*, 19 (June): 694-709.

141. "A Second Lecture on the Fine Arts, by Michael Angelo Titmarsh, Esq. The Exhibitions." *Fraser's Magazine*, 19 (June): 743-50.

142. "Catherine: A Story [Chaps. V-VI]. By Ikey Solomons, Esq. Junior."
With an illustration. *Fraser's Magazine*, 20 (July): 98-112.

143. "Illustrations of the Rent Laws.—No. I." [A drawing with letter-press.] *The Anti-Corn Law Circular*, No. 8 (23 July): [iv].
(Cole, 2: 143-46)

144. "Catherine: A Story [Chap. VII]. By Ikey Solomons, Esq. Junior."
With an illustration. *Fraser's Magazine*, 20 (Aug.): 224-32.

145. "Captain Rook and Mr. Pigeon. By William Thacker[a]y." *Heads of the People Taken Off by Kenny Meadows*. [With two illustrations by Meadows.] First Series. No. X (Aug.): 305-20.

146. "Letters from London, Paris, Pekin, Petersburgh, &c. By the au-thor of 'The Yellowplush Correspondence,' the 'Memoirs of Major Gahagan,' &c." Signed "T. T." *The Corsair* [New York], 24 Aug., pp. 380-82.   (*Paris Sketch Book*: "An Invasion of France.")

147. "Letters from London, Paris, Pekin, Petersburgh, &c. By the au-thor of 'The Yellowplush Correspondence,' the 'Memoirs of Major Gahagan,' &c." Signed "T. T." *The Corsair* [New York], 14 Sept., pp. 429-30. (*Paris Sketch Book*: "Madame Sand and the New Apocalypse.")

148. "Letters from London, Paris, Pekin, Petersburgh, &c. By the au-thor of 'The Yellowplush Correspondence,' the 'Memoirs of Major Gahagan,' &c. (Madame Sand and Spiridion Concluded.)" Signed "T. T." *The Corsair* [New York], 21 Sept., pp. 445-47.
(*Paris Sketch Book*: "Madame Sand and the New Apocalypse.")

149. "Letters from London, Paris, Pekin, Petersburgh, &c. By the au-thor of 'The Yellowplush Correspondence,' the 'Memoirs of Major Gahagan,' &c." Signed "T. T." *The Corsair* [New York], 5 Oct., pp. 473-75. (*Paris Sketch Book*: "The Fêtes of July.")

150. "The French Plutarch. No. I. I. Cartouche. II. Poinsinet." *Fraser's Magazine*, 20 (Oct.): 447-59.   (*Paris Sketch Book*)

151. "Letters from London, Paris, Pekin, Petersburgh, &c. By the au-thor of 'The Yellowplush Correspondence,' the 'Memoirs of Major Gahagan,' &c." Signed "T. T." *The Corsair* [New York], 26 Oct., pp. 521-23.

152. "Catherine: A Story [Chaps. VIII-X]. By Ikey Solomons, Esq. Jun-ior." *Fraser's Magazine*, 20 (Nov.): 531-48.

153. "On the French School of Painting." Signed "M. A. T." *Fraser's Magazine*, 20 (Dec.): 679-88.   (*Paris Sketch Book*)

154. "The Great Cossack Epic of Demetrius Rigmarolovicz." *Fraser's Magazine*, 20 (Dec.): 715-27.
>> (*Miscellanies*: "The Legend of St. Sophia of Kioff")

155. "Illustrations of the Rent Laws.—No. II. British Independence, or The Choice of a Loaf." [A drawing with letterpress.] *The Anti-Corn Law Circular*, No. 18 (10 Dec.): [iv].   (Cole, 2: 143-46)

156. "Barber Cox and the Cutting of his Comb." *The Comic Almanack for 1840, With Twelve Illustrations of the Months, by Geo. Cruikshank.* London: Charles Tilt, [1839], pp. 4-5. 8-9, 12-13, 16-17, 20-21, 24-25, 28-29, 32-33, 36-37, 40-41, 44-45, 48.

157. [Four illustrations to John Barrow. *The Exquisites: A Farce in Two Acts.* (For private circulation only.) London: privately printed, 1839.]

1840

158. "Epistles to the Literati. No. XIII. Ch—s Y-ll-wpl-sh, Esq. to Sir Edward Lytton Bulwer, Bart." *Fraser's Magazine*, 21 (Jan.): 71-80.

159. "Catherine: A Story [Chaps. XI-XIII]. By Ikey Solomons, Esq. Junior." *Fraser's Magazine*, 21 (Jan.): 106-15.

160. "The Bedford-Row Conspiracy. In Two Parts." *The New Monthly Magazine*, 108 (Jan.): 99-111.

161. "Catherine: A Story [Chaps. (XIV)-(XV)]. By Ikey Solomons, Esq. Junior." *Fraser's Magazine*, 21 (Feb.): 200-12.

162. "The Fashionable Authoress. By William Thackeray." *Heads of the People or Portraits of the English.* [With an illustration by Kenny Meadows.] New Series. No. III (Feb.): 73-84.

163. "Epistles to the Literati. No. XIV. On French Criticism of the English, and Notably in the Affair of the Vengeur." *Fraser's Magazine*, 21 (Mar.): 332-45.   (*Letters*, 1: cvii)

164. "The Bedford-Row Conspiracy. Part Two. Chap. I." *The New Monthly Magazine*, 108 (Mar.): 416-25.

165. "Krasinski's Sketch of the Reformation in Poland.—Vol. II." *The Times*, 5 Mar., p. 5.   (*Letters*, 1: 424-25)

166. "Turnbull's Austria." *The Times*, 16 Mar., p. 3.   (*Letters [H]*, 1: 60)

167. "The Bedford-Row Conspiracy. Part Two. Chap. II." *The New Monthly Magazine*, 108 (Apr.): 547-57.

168. "The Artists. By Michael Angelo Titmarsh." *Heads of the People or Portraits of the English*. [With two illustrations by Kenny Meadows.] New Series. No. VI (May): 161-76.

169. "A Shabby Genteel Story [Chaps. I-II]." *Fraser's Magazine*, 21 (June): 677-89.

170. "A Pictorial Rhapsody by Michael Angelo Titmarsh." *Fraser's Magazine*, 21 (June): 720-32.

171. "George Cruikshank." Signed "Ø." *The Westminster Review*, 34 (June): 1-60.

172. "Ranke's 'History of the Popes.' " *The Times*, 10 June, p. 3.
(*Letters*, 1: 460-61)

173. "A Shabby Genteel Story [Chaps. III-IV]." *Fraser's Magazine*, 22 (July): 90-101.

174. "A Pictorial Rhapsody: Concluded." *Fraser's Magazine*, 22 (July): 112-26.

175. Illustration entitled "Give Us Our Daily Bread." *The Anti-Corn Law Circular*, No. 39 (30 July): [iii].   (*Letters [H]*, 1: 50-51)

176. "Going to See A Man Hanged." Signed "W. M. T." With an illustration. *Fraser's Magazine*, 22 (Aug.): 150-58.

177. "A Shabby Genteel Story [Chaps. V-VI]." *Fraser's Magazine*, 22 (Aug.): 226-37.

178. "Ranke's 'History of the Popes.' " *The Times*, 11 Aug., p. 6.

179. "Ranke's 'History of the Popes.' " *The Times*, 18 Aug., p. 6.

180. "Fielding's Works. In One Volume. With a Memoir by Thomas Roscoe." *The Times*, 2 Sept., p. 6.

181. "A Shabby Genteel Story [Chaps. VII-IX]." *Fraser's Magazine*, 22 (Oct.): 399-414.

1841

182. "Gisquet's Memoirs." *Fraser's Magazine*, 23 (May): 584-93.
(Stokes, pp. 281-82)

183. "Loose Sketches. By Mr. Michael Angelo Titmarsh. [Reading a Poem.] In Two Parts.—Part I." *Britannia*, 1 May, pp. 283-84.

184. "Loose Sketches. By Mr. Michael Angelo Titmarsh. Reading a Poem. In Two Parts.—Part II." *Britannia*, 8 May, pp. 299-300.

185. "Loose Sketches. By Mr. Michael Angelo Titmarsh. A St. Philip's Day at Paris." *Britannia*, 15 May, pp. 315-16.

186. "Loose Sketches. By Mr. Michael Angelo Titmarsh. St. Philip's Day at Paris." *Britannia*, 22 May, p. 330.

187. "Memorials of Gormandising. In a Letter to Oliver Yorke, Esq. by M. A. Titmarsh." *Fraser's Magazine*, 23 (June): 710-25.

188. "Loose Sketches. By Mr. Michael Angelo Titmarsh. Shrove Tuesday in Paris." *Britannia*, 5 June, p. 363.

189. "Loose Sketches. By Mr. Michael Angelo Titmarsh. Rolandseck." *Britannia*, 19 June, p. 394.

190. "On Men and Pictures." *Fraser's Magazine*, 24 (July): 98-111.
    (Letters, 2: 19)

191. "The Firebrand Correspondence." [A broadside.] *(Letters [H]*, 2: 843)

192. "Men and Coats." *Fraser's Magazine*, 24 (Aug.): 208-17.
    (Letters, 2: 33)

193. "The History of Samuel Titmarsh and the Great Hoggarty Diamond [Chaps. I-V]." *Fraser's Magazine*, 24 (Sept.): 324-43.

194. "Notes on the North What-d'ye-callem Election [Letters I-II]." *Fraser's Magazine*, 24 (Sept.): 352-58.   *(Letters*, 2: 33)

195. "The History of Samuel Titmarsh and the Great Hoggarty Diamond [Chaps. VI-VII]." *Fraser's Magazine*, 24 (Oct.): 389-99.

196. "Notes on the North What-d'ye-callem Election [Letters III-IV]." *Fraser's Magazine*, 24 (Oct.): 413-27.

197. "Little Spitz. A Lenten Anecdote, from the German of Professor Spass. By Michael Angelo Titmarsh." [With an illustration by George Cruikshank.] *George Cruikshank's Omnibus*, 1 (Oct.): 167-72.

198. "The History of Samuel Titmarsh and the Great Hoggarty Diamond [Chaps. VIII-X]." *Fraser's Magazine*, 24 (Nov.): 594-611.

199. "The History of Samuel Titmarsh and the Great Hoggarty Diamond [Chaps. XI-XIII]." *Fraser's Magazine*, 24 (Dec.): 717-34.

200. "The King of Brentford's Testament. By Michael Angelo Titmarsh." *George Cruikshank's Omnibus*, 1 (Dec.): 244-46.

1842

201. "Sultan Stork. Being the One Thousand and Second Night. Translated from the Persian, by Major G. O'Gahagan, H. E. I. C. S. Part the First.—The Magic Powder." [With an illustration by George Cruikshank.] *Ainsworth's Magazine*, 1 (Feb.): 33-38.

202. "Dickens in France." With two illustrations. *Fraser's Magazine*, 25 (Mar.): 342-52. *(Letters, 2: 45)*

203. "The Rhine [by Victor Hugo]." *The Foreign Quarterly Review*, 29 (Apr.): 139-67. *(Letters, 2: 44, 830)*

204. "Sultan Stork. Being the One Thousand and Second Night. Translated from the Persian, by Major G. O'Gahagan, H. E. I. C. S. Part the Second.—The Enchanted Princess." [With an illustration by George Cruikshank.] *Ainsworth's Magazine*, 1 (May): 233-37.

205. "Fitz-Boodle's Confessions. George Fitz-Boodle, Esquire, to Oliver Yorke, Esquire." *Fraser's Magazine*, 25 (June): 707-21.

206. "An Exhibition Gossip. By Michael Angelo Titmarsh." *Ainsworth's Magazine*, 1 (June): 319-22. *(Letters, 2: 54)*

207. ["The Legend of Jawbrahim-Heraudee." With four illustrations. *Punch*, 2 (18 June): 254-56.] *(Spielmann, pp. 16-17, 319)*

208. "Professions by George Fitz-Boodle. Being Appeals to the Unemployed Younger Sons of the Nobility." *Fraser's Magazine*, 26 (July): 43-60.

209. "The German in England." *The Foreign Quarterly Review*, 29 (July): 370-83. *(Letters, 2: 70)*

210. "The Last Fifteen Years of the Bourbons." *The Foreign Quarterly Review*, 29 (July): 384-420. *(Letters, 2: 70)*

211. "Miss Tickletoby's Lectures on English History. A Character, (To Introduce Another Character)." With two illustrations. *Punch*, 3 (2 July): 8-9.

212. "Miss Tickletoby's Lecture." With an illustration. *Punch*, 3 (9 July): 12-13.

213. "Miss Tickletoby's Lectures on English History. Miss Tickletoby's Second Lecture. The Picts, the Scots, the Danes; Gregory the Satirist, The Conversion of the Britons, The Character of Alfred." With two illustrations. *Punch*, 3 (16 July): 28-30.

214. "Miss Tickletoby's Lectures on English History. Lecture III.—The Sea-Kings in England." With two illustrations. *Punch*, 3 (6 Aug.): 58-59.

215. "Miss Tickletoby's Lectures on English History. Lecture IV.—Edward the Confessor.—Harold.—William the Conqueror." With two illustrations. *Punch*, 3 (13 Aug.): 70-72.

216. "Miss Tickletoby's Lectures on English History. Lecture V.—William Rufus." With two illustrations. *Punch*, 3 (20 Aug.): 84-85.

217. "Miss Tickletoby's Lectures on English History. Lecture VI.—Henry I.—Maude.—Stephen.—Henry II." With an illustration. *Punch*, 3 (27 Aug.): 91-92.

218. "Miss Tickletoby's Lectures on English History. Richard the First." With three illustrations. *Punch*, 3 (10 Sept.): 116-17.

219. "Miss Tickletoby's Lectures on English History. [John.—Henry III.—Edward I.]" With two illustrations. *Punch*, 3 (17 Sept.): 121-22.

220. "Miss Tickletoby's Lectures on English History. Edward I.—The Scots and Their Claims." With three illustrations. *Punch*, 3 (24 Sept.): 131-33.

221. "Miss Tickletoby's Lectures on English History. Edward III." With three illustrations. *Punch*, 3 (1 Oct.): 142-43.

222. "Fitz-Boodle's Confessions. Miss Löwe." *Fraser's Magazine*, 26 (Oct.): 395-405.

223. "Travelling Romancers: Dumas on the Rhine." *The Foreign Quarterly Review*, 30 (Oct.): 105-24.   (*Letters [H]*, 2: 121-22)

1843

224. "Confessions of George Fitz-Boodle. Dorothea." *Fraser's Magazine*, 27 (Jan.): 76-84.

225. ["The Sick Child. By the Honourable Wilhelmina Skeggs." (With an Iillustration by John Leech.) *Punch*, 4 (14 Jan.): 30.]
                                        (Spielmann, pp. 34, 320)

226. "Confessions of George Fitz-Boodle. Ottilia." *Fraser's Magazine*, 27 (Feb.): 214-24.

227. "Mr. Spec's Remonstrance." With two illustrations. *Punch*, 4 (11 Feb.): 69-70.

228. "Confessions of George Fitz-Boodle. Men's Wives. [No. I.] Mr. and Mrs. Frank Berry." With an illustration. *Fraser's Magazine*, 27 (Mar.): 349-61.

229. "Letters on the Fine Arts. No. 1. The Art Unions. From M. A. Titmarsh, Esq., to Sanders McGilp, Esq." *The Pictorial Times*, 1 (18 Mar.): 13-14.

230. Signed illustration to "The Cabinet and Colonel Sibthorp." *Punch*, 4 (25 Mar.): 126.

231. "Confessions of George Fitz-Boodle. Men's Wives. No. II. The Ravenswing [Chap. I]." *Fraser's Magazine*, 27 (Apr.): 465-75.

232. "George Herwegh's Poems." *The Foreign Quarterly Review*, 31 (Apr.): 58-72.   (*Letters [H]*, 2: 127-28)

233. "Thieves' Literature of France." *The Foreign Quarterly Review*, 31 (Apr.): 231-49.   (*Letters*, 2: 92)

234. "Letters on the Fine Arts. No. 2. The Objections Against Art Unions. M. A. Titmarsh, Esq., to Sanders McGilp, Esq." *The Pictorial Times*, 1 (1 Apr.): 43.

235. ["Mr. Macaulay's Essays." *The Pictorial Times*, 1 (1 Apr.): 43.]

236. "Letters on the Fine Arts. No. 2. The Objections Against Art Unions. M. A. Titmarsh, Esq., to Sanders McGilp, Esq." *The Pictorial Times*, 1 (8 Apr.): 61-62.

237. Signed illustration to "The Astley-Napoleon Museum." *Punch*, 4 (29 Apr.): 176.

238. Signed illustration to "To Persons in Want of a Brougham." *Punch*, 4 (29 Apr.): 182.

239. "Men's Wives. By George Fitz-Boodle. No. II. The Ravenswing [Chaps. II-III]." *Fraser's Magazine*, 27 (May): 597-608.

240. "The Water Colour Exhibitions." Signed "Michael Angelo Titmarsh." *The Pictorial Times*, 1 (6 May): 125.

241. "Letters on the Fine Arts. No. 3. The Royal Academy." Signed "M. A. Titmarsh." *The Pictorial Times*, 1 (13 May): 136-37.

242. "A Turkish Letter concerning the Divertissement 'Les Houris.'" With two illustrations, one signed. *Punch*, 4 (13 May): 199.
           (Spielmann, p. 320)

243. "Daddy, I'm Hungry. A Scene in an Irish Coachmaker's Family, Designed by Lord Lowther, July, 1843." With an illustration. *The Nation* (Dublin), 13 May, p. 492.　　　　　　(Benjamin, 2: 186)

244. Illustration to "Assumption of Aristocracy." *Punch*, 4 (20 May): 204.　　　　　　(Spielmann, p. 320)

245. "Second Turkish Letter concerning the Divertissement 'Les Houris.'" With an illustration. *Punch*, 4 (20 May): 209.
　　　　　　(Spielmann, p. 320)

246. "Letters on the Fine Arts.—No. IV. The Royal Academy—(Second Notice)." Signed "M. A. Titmarsh." *The Pictorial Times*, 1 (27 May): 169-70.

247. "Men's Wives. By George Fitz-Boodle. No. II. The Ravenswing [Chap. (IV)]." *Fraser's Magazine*, 27 (June): 723-33.

248. Signed illustration to "Sale of Miscellaneous Furniture." *Punch*, 5 (8 July): 20.

249. "Men's Wives. By George Fitz-Boodle. No. II. The Ravenswing [Chaps. V-VI]." *Fraser's Magazine*, 28 (Aug.): 188-205.

250. "Men's Wives. By George Fitz-Boodle. No. II. The Ravenswing [Chaps. VII-VIII]." *Fraser's Magazine*, 28 (Sept.): 321-37.

251. "Jerome Paturot. With Considerations on Novels in General—In a Letter from M. A. Titmarsh." *Fraser's Magazine*, 28 (Sept.): 349-62.

252. "Bluebeard's Ghost. By M. A. Titmarsh." *Fraser's Magazine*, 28 (Oct.): 413-25.

253. "Men's Wives. By George Fitz-Boodle. No. III. Dennis Haggarty's Wife." *Fraser's Magazine*, 28 (Oct.): 494-504.

254. "Death and Dying in France." *The Foreign Quarterly Review*, 32 (Oct.): 76-89.　　　　　　(*Letters [H]*, 2: 132)

255. ["French Romancers on England." *The Foreign Quarterly Review*, 32 (Oct.): 226-46.]　　　　(*Adversity*, p. 485; *Wellesley*, 2: 166)

256. Signed illustration to "Recollections of the Opera." *Punch*, 5 (28 Oct.): 184.

257. "Men's Wives. By George Fitz-Boodle. No. IV. The——'s Wife." *Fraser's Magazine*, 28 (Nov.): 581-92.

258. Two illustrations, one signed, to "The Flying Duke." *Punch*, 5 (11 Nov.): 207.

259. "Grant in Paris. By G. S. F. B." *Fraser's Magazine*, 28 (Dec.): 702-12.

260. Two illustrations, one signed, to "Punch's Condensed Magazine." *Punch*, 5 (9 Dec.): 254.

261. "Singular Letter from the Regent of Spain." With three illustrations, one signed. *Punch*, 5 (16 Dec.): 267-68. (Spielmann, p. 320)

1844

262. "The Luck of Barry Lyndon; A Romance of the Last Century [Chaps. I-II]. By Fitz-Boodle." *Fraser's Magazine*, 29 (Jan.): 35-51.

263. "New Accounts of Paris." *The Foreign Quarterly Review*, 32 (Jan.): 470-90.   (*Letters*, 2: 126)

264. "Important Promotions! Merit Rewarded!" With an illustration. *Punch*, 6 (6 Jan.): 15.   (Spielmann, p. 320)

265. "The Ducal Hat for Jenkins." With three illustrations. *Punch*, 6 (13 Jan.): 32.   (Spielmann, p. 320)

266. "Leaves from the Lives of the Lords of Literature." With a Notice and two illustrations. *Punch*, 6 (20 Jan.): 42. (Spielmann, p. 320)

267. "Lady L.'s Journal of a Visit to Foreign Courts." [With two illustrations probably not by Thackeray.] *Punch*, 6 (27 Jan.): 52-54.
(Spielmann, p. 320)

268. "A Box of Novels." Signed "M. A. T." *Fraser's Magazine*, 29 (Feb.): 153-69.

269. "The Luck of Barry Lyndon; A Romance of the Last Century [Chaps. III-IV]. By Fitz-Boodle." *Fraser's Magazine*, 29 (Feb.): 187-202.

270. "The History of the Next French Revolution! From a forthcoming History of Europe. Chapter I." [With an illustration probably not by Thackeray.] *Punch*, 6 (24 Feb.): 90, 93.

271. "The Luck of Barry Lyndon; A Romance of the Last Century [Chaps. V-VI]. By Fitz-Boodle." *Fraser's Magazine*, 29 (Mar.): 318-30.

272. "Titmarsh's Carmen Lilliense." *Fraser's Magazine*, 29 (Mar.): 361-63.   (*Miscellanies*)

273. "The History of the Next French Revolution. From a forthcoming History of Europe. Chap. II.—Henry V and Napoleon III." [With an illustration probably not by Thackeray.] *Punch*, 6 (2 Mar.): 98-99.

274. "The History of the Next French Revolution. From a forthcoming History of Europe. Chap. III.—The Advance of the Pretenders— Historical Review." [With two illustrations probably not by Thackeray.] *Punch*, 6 (9 Mar.): 113-14.

275. "The History of the Next French Revolution. From a forthcoming History of Europe. Chap. IV.—The Battle of Rheims." [With an illustration probably not by Thackeray.] *Punch*, 6 (16 Mar): 117.

276. [*"Ireland.* By J. Venedey." *The Morning Chronicle*, 16 Mar., p. 6.]
(*Letters*, 2: 143)

277. ["(Madden's) *Ireland and its Rulers, since 1829,*" *The Morning Chronicle*, 20 Mar., p. 5.] ("Chronicle")

278. "The History of the Next French Revolution. From a forthcoming History of Europe. Chap. V.—The Battle of Tours." [With two illustrations probably not by Thackeray.] *Punch*, 6 (23 Mar.): 127-28.

279. "Biographical and Literary Riddles." *Punch*, 6 (23 Mar.): 129.
(Spielmann, p. 320)

280. "'The Author of Pelham.'" *Punch*, 6 (23 Mar.): 130.
(Spielmann, p. 320)

281. "The History of the Next French Revolution. From a forthcoming History of Europe. Chap. VI.—The English Under Jenkins." [With two illustrations probably not by Thackeray.] *Punch*, 6 (30 Mar.): 137-39.

282. "The Luck of Barry Lyndon; A Romance of the Last Century [Chaps. VII-IX]. By Fitz-Boodle." *Fraser's Magazine*, 29 (Apr.): 391-410.

283. "*A New Spirit of the Age*, edited by R. H. Horne." *The Morning Chronicle*, 2 Apr., p. 6. ("Chronicle")

284. [*"The Three Kingdoms*, By the Vicomte D'Arlincourt." *The Morning Chronicle*, 4 Apr., p. 3.] ("Chronicle")

285. "The History of the Next French Revolution. From a forthcoming History of Europe. Chap. VII.—The Leaguer of Paris." [With two illustrations probably not by Thackeray.] *Punch*, 6 (6 Apr.): 147-48.

286. "Gems from Jenkins." *Punch*, 6 (6 Apr.): 153. (Spielmann, p. 321)

287. "What Should Irish Members Do in Regard to the Ten Hours' Bill?" *Punch*, 6 (6 Apr.): 155. (Spielmann, p. 321)

288. "The History of the Next French Revolution. From a forthcoming History of Europe. Chap. VIII.—The Battle of the Forts." [With an illustration probably not by Thackeray.] *Punch*, 6 (13 Apr.): 157.

289. "An Eligible Investment." With an illustration. *Punch*, 6 (13 Apr.): 164. (Spielmann, p. 321)

290. "The History of the Next French Revolution. From a forthcoming History of Europe. Chap. IX.—Louis XVII." [With two illustrations probably not by Thackeray.] *Punch*, 6 (20 Apr.): 167-68.

291. "Les Premières Armes de Montpensier; or, Munchausen Outdone." With two illustrations. *Punch*, 6 (27 Apr.): 184.
(Spielmann, p. 321)

292. ["Exhibition of the Society of Painters in Water Colours." *The Morning Chronicle*, 29 Apr., p. 6.] ("Chronicle")

293. "Little Travels and Road-side Sketches. By Titmarsh. [No. I.] From Richmond in Surrey to Brussels in Belgium." *Fraser's Magazine*, 29 (May): 517-28.

294. "The Luck of Barry Lyndon; A Romance of the Last Century [Chaps. X-XI]. By Fitz-Boodle." *Fraser's Magazine*, 29 (May): 548-63.

295. "The Partie Fine. By Lancelot Wagstaff, Esq." *The New Monthly Magazine*, 71 (May): 22-28.

296. "Great News! Wonderful News!" With an illustration. *Punch*, 6 (4 May): 189. (Spielmann, p. 321)

297. ["*The Life of George Brummell, Esq.*, By Captain Jesse." *The Morning Chronicle*, 6 May, p. 5.] ("Chronicle")

298. "Academy Exhibition." [With an illustration by H. C. Hine.] *Punch*, 6 (11 May): 200. (Spielmann, p. 321)

299. "A Rare New Ballad of Malbrook, To a New Tune. To be Sung at Woodstock, at the Election Dinners There." *Punch*, 6 (11 May): 207. (Spielmann, p. 321)

300. ["*Coningsby; or, the New Generation.*" *The Morning Chronicle*, 13 May, p. 5.] ("Chronicle")

301. [*"Coningsby; or the New Generation*. By B. D'Israeli, Esq., M.P." *The Pictorial Times*, 3 (25 May): 331.]

302. "The Clocks Again." *Punch*, 6 (25 May): 227. (Spielmann, p. 321)

303. "Latest from America. Animated Discussion of the Pork and Molasses Bill.—Glorious Discomfiture of Jer. Diddler's Party." With an illustration. *Punch*, 6 (25 May): 228.   (Spielmann, p. 321)

304. "May Gambols; or, Titmarsh in the Picture-Galleries." *Fraser's Magazine*, 29 (June): 700-16.

305. "The Luck of Barry Lyndon; A Romance of the Last Century [Chaps. XII-XIII]. By Fitz-Boodle." *Fraser's Magazine*, 29 (June): 723-38.

306. "Arabella; or, The Moral of 'The Partie Fine.' " Signed "Titmarsh." *The New Monthly Magazine*, 71 (June): 169-72.

307. "The Prince of Joinville's Amateur-Invasion of England." [With an illustration probably not by Thackeray.] *Punch*, 6 (1 June): 234, 237.   (Spielmann, p. 321)

308. ["Stanley's *Life of Dr. Arnold*." *The Morning Chronicle*, 3 June, p. 3.]
                                                        ("Chronicle")

309. "Rules To be observed by the English People on occasion of the Visit of his Imperial Majesty, Nicholas, Emperor of all the Russias." [With an illustration probably not by Thackeray.] *Punch*, 6 (8 June): 243.   (Spielmann, p. 321)

310. "Strange Insult to the King of Saxony." *Punch*, 6 (8 June): 243.
                                                        (Spielmann, p. 321)

311. "To Daniel O'Connell, Esq. Circular Road, Dublin." *Punch*, 6 (8 June): 248.   (Spielmann, p. 321)

312. "The Dream of Joinville." [With an illustration probably not by Thackeray.] *Punch*, 6 (15 June): 252.   (Spielmann, p. 321)

313. "Punch to the Public. Private and Confidential." *Punch*, 7 (29 June): 4.   (Spielmann, p. 321)

314. "The Luck of Barry Lyndon; A Romance of the Last Century [Chaps. XIV-XV]. By Fitz-Boodle." *Fraser's Magazine*, 30 (July): 93-108.

315. "Angleterre. Par Alfred Michiels." *The Foreign Quarterly Review*, 33 (July): 433-42.   (*Adversity*, p. 485; *Wellesley*, 2: 168)

316. "Greenwich—Whitebait. By Mr. Wagstaff." *The New Monthly Magazine*, 71 (July): 416-21.

317. "A Hint for Moses." With two illustrations. *Punch*, 7 (6 July): 19.
(Spielmann, p. 321)

318. "A Nut for the Paris Charivari." *Punch*, 7 (6 July): 19.
(Spielmann, p. 321)

319. "Interesting Meeting." *Punch*, 7 (6 July): 22. (Spielmann, p. 322)

320. "Running Rein Morality." *Punch*, 7 (13 July): 23. (Spielmann, p. 322)

321. "Punch's Fine Art Exhibition." With an illustration [and ten by John Leech]. *Punch*, 7 (13 July): 26. (Spielmann, p. 322)

322. "A Case of Real Distress." *Punch*, 7 (13 July): 32. With an illustration. (Spielmann, p. 322)

323. "Moorish Designs." *Punch*, 7 (13 July): 32. (Spielmann, p. 322)

324. "Punch to Daniel in Prison." [With an illustration by John Leech.] *Punch*, 7 (20 July): 38. (Spielmann, p. 322)

325. "Literary Intelligence." *Punch*, 7 (20 July): 42. (Spielmann, p. 322)

326. "Irish Razors." *Punch*, 7 (20 July): 44. (Spielmann, p. 322)

327. "The Luck of Barry Lyndon; A Romance of the Last Century [Chaps. XVI-XVII]. By Fitz-Boodle." *Fraser's Magazine*, 30 (Aug.): 227-42.

328. ["*Historic Fancies.* By the Hon. George Sidney Smythe, M.P." *The Morning Chronicle*, 2 Aug., p. 5.] (*Letters*, 2: 145)

329. "Wanderings of Our Fat Contributor." With two illustrations [and one probably not by Thackeray]. *Punch*, 7 (3 Aug.): 61-62.

330. "Travelling Notes. By Our Fat Contributor. The Sea." *Punch*, 7 (10 Aug.): 66-67.

331. "Travelling Notes. By Our Fat Contributor. The Sea." With three illustrations. *Punch*, 7 (17 Aug.): 83-84.

332. "A Chance Lost." *Punch*, 7 (17 Aug.): 85. (Spielmann, p. 322)

333. "To the Napoleon of Peace." [With an illustration probably not by Thackeray.] *Punch*, 7 (24 Aug.): 90. (Spielmann, p. 322)

334. "Fashionable Removals." *Punch*, 7 (24 Aug.): 94. (Spielmann, p. 322)

335. "Revolution in France." [With an illustration probably not by Thackeray.] *Punch*, 7 (24 Aug.): 95.   (Spielmann, p. 322)

336. "The Last Insult to Poor Old Ireland." *Punch*, 7 (24 Aug.): 95.
     (Spielmann, p. 322)

337. "Jenny Wren's Remonstrance." [With an illustration probably not by Thackeray.] *Punch*, 7 (24 Aug.): 96.   (Spielmann, p. 322)

338. "The Luck of Barry Lyndon; A Romance of the Last Century. Part II [Chap. I]. By Fitz-Boodle." *Fraser's Magazine*, 30 (Sept.): 353-64.

339. "The Wooden-Shoe and the Buffalo-Indians." With an illustration. *Punch*, 7 (7 Sept.): 110.   (Spielmann, p. 322)

340. "Shameful Case of Letter Opening. A Tale of the British and Foreign Institute." With two illustrations. *Punch*, 7 (7 Sept.): 117.
     (Spielmann, p. 322)

341. "Letters from a Club Arm-Chair." Signed "Squab." *The Calcutta Star*, 21 Sept.   (Summerfield, p. 43)

342. "Little Travels and Road-Side Sketches. By Titmarsh. No. II.—Ghent—Bruges." *Fraser's Magazine*, 30 (Oct.): 465-71.

343. "The Luck of Barry Lyndon; A Romance of the Last Century. Part II [Chap. II]. By Fitz-Boodle." *Fraser's Magazine*, 30 (Nov.): 584-97.

344. "Travelling Notes by Our Fat Contributor." With two illustrations. *Punch*, 7 (30 Nov.): 237.

345. "The Luck of Barry Lyndon; A Romance of the Last Century. Part II [Chap. III]. By Fitz-Boodle." *Fraser's Magazine*, 30 (Dec.): 666-83.

346. "Travelling Notes by Our Fat Contributor. II.—The Ship at Sea.—Dolores!" With three illustrations. *Punch*, 7 (7 Dec.): 256-57.

347. "Travelling Notes by Our Fat Contributor. III. From my Log-book at Sea." With four illustrations. *Punch*, 7 (14 Dec.): 265-66.

1845

348. "Little Travels and Road-Side Sketches. By Titmarsh. Waterloo. No. III." *Fraser's Magazine*, 31 (Jan.): 94-96.

349. "Punch in the East. From Our Fat Contributor." With two illustrations. *Punch*, 8 (11 Jan.): 31-32.

350. "Punch in the East. From Our Fat Contributor. II.—On the Prospects of Punch in the East." With two illustrations. *Punch*, 8 (18 Jan.): 35-36.

351. "Punch in the East. From Our Fat Contributor. III. Athens." With three illustrations. *Punch*, 8 (25 Jan.): 45.

352. "Punch in the East. By Our Fat Contributor. IV.—Punch at the Pyramids." With two illustrations. *Punch*, 8 (1 Feb.): 61.

353. "Punch in the East. By Our Fat Contributor. V.—Punch at the Pyramids—(Concluded)." With an illustration. *Punch*, 8 (8 Feb.): 75.

354. "The Honour of the Bar." *Punch*, 8 (22 March): 129.

(Spielmann, p. 322)

355. ["*Egypt Under Mehemet Ali*. By Prince Puckler Muskau." *The Morning Chronicle*, 27 Mar., p. 5.] ("Chronicle")

356. ["Polk's First Address." *The Examiner*, 29 Mar., p. 194.]

(*Letters*, 2: 190)

357. ["Mount Sorel." *The Examiner*, 29 Mar., pp. 196-97.] (*Letters*, 2: 190)

358. "Disgusting Violation of the Rights of Property." *Punch*, 8 (29 March): 142. (Spielmann, p. 322)

359. "Historical Parallel." *Punch*, 8 (29 Mar.): 149. (Spielmann, p. 322)

360. ["Lever's *St. Patrick's Eve*—Comic Politics." *The Morning Chronicle*, 3 Apr., pp. 5-6.] ("Chronicle")

361. "Liberal Reward." With an illustration. *Punch*, 8 (5 Apr.): 151.

(Spielmann, p. 323)

362. "Mr. Smith's Reasons for Not Sending His Pictures to the Exhibition. [With an illustration probably not by Thackeray.] *Punch*, 8 (5 Apr.): 152. (Spielmann, p. 323)

363. "Genteel Christianity." *Punch*, 8 (5 Apr.): 153. (Spielmann, p. 323)

364. "A Painter's Wish." Signed "Paul Pindar." *Punch*, 8 (5 Apr.): 154.

(Spielmann, p. 323)

365. "Dog Annexation." [With an illustration probably not by Thackeray.] *Punch*, 8 (5 Apr.): 159. (Spielmann, p. 323)

366. "The '82 Club Uniform." *Punch*, 8 (5 April): 159. (Spielmann, p. 323)

367. "For the Court Circular." *Punch*, 8 (12 Apr.): 167.

(Spielmann, p. 323)

368. "Royal Patronage of Art." *Punch*, 8 (12 Apr.): 167.

(Spielmann, p. 323)

369. "The Irish Martyrs." *Punch*, 8 (12 Apr.): 168. (Spielmann, p. 323)

370. "Erratum." *Punch,* 8 (12 Apr.): 170. (Spielmann, p. 323)

371. "Gross Insult to the Court." *Punch,* 8 (12 Apr.): 170.
(Spielmann, p. 323)

372. "The Commission of Fine Arts." *Punch,* 8 (19 Apr.): 172.
(Spielmann, p. 323)

373. "Literary News." *Punch,* 8 (26 Apr.): 184. (Spielmann, p. 323)

374. "Ode to Sibthorpe, by the Poet Laureate." With an illustration.
Punch, 8 (26 Apr.): 188. (Spielmann, p. 323)

375. "Humours of the House of Commons." *Punch,* 8 (26 Apr.): 190.
(Spielmann, p. 323)

376. "You're Another." *Punch,* 8 (26 April): 190. (Spielmann, p. 323)

377. "The Excellent New Ballad of Mr. Peel at Toledo." *Punch,* 8
(3 May): 195. (Spielmann, p. 323)

378. "Letters from a Club Arm-Chair." Signed "Squab." *The Calcutta Star,*
7 May. (Summerfield, p. 43)

379. "Delightful Novelty." *Punch,* 8 (10 May): 205. (Spielmann, p. 323)

380. "New Portrait of H.R.H. Prince Albert." With two illustrations.
Punch, 8 (10 May): 211. (Spielmann, p. 323)

381. "*Sibyl.* By Mr. Disraeli, M.P." *The Morning Chronicle,* 13 May, pp. 5-6.
(*Letters,* 2: 149n)

382. "The Queen's *Bal Costumé,* or, Powder and Ball." With an illustration. *Punch,* 8 (17 May): 219. (Spielmann, p. 323)

383. "Peel at Toledo." *Punch,* 8 (17 May): 220. (Spielmann, p. 323)

384. "Letters from a Club Arm-Chair." Signed "Squab." *The Calcutta Star,*
22 May. (Summerfield, p. 43)

385. "Mr. Punch on the Fine Arts." [With an illustration by Richard
Doyle.] *Punch,* 8 (24 May): 224. (Spielmann, p. 323)

386. "Father Mathew's Debts." *Punch,* 8 (24 May): 232.
(Spielmann, p. 323)

387. "Split in Conciliation Hall." *Punch,* 8 (31 May): 243.
(Spielmann, p. 323)

388. "Preparations for War." *Punch,* 8 (31 May): 243. (Spielmann, p. 323)

389. "The Allegory of the Fountains." *Punch,* 8 (31 May): 243.
(Spielmann, p. 323)

390. "Railroad Speculators." Signed "Spec." With an illustration. *Punch,* 8 (31 May): 244.

391. "Picture Gossip: In a Letter from Michael Angelo Titmarsh." *Fraser's Magazine,* 31 (June): 713-24.

392. "A Legend of the Rhine [Chaps. I-II]." [With three illustrations by Cruikshank.] *George Cruikshank's Table-Book,* No. 6 (June): 119-25.

393. "Her Majesty's *Bal Poudre.*" *Punch,* 8 (7 June): 251.
(Spielmann, p. 323)

394. "Letters from a Club Arm-Chair." Signed "Squab." *The Calcutta Star,* 9 June.
(Summerfield, p. 43)

395. "Young Ireland." With an illustration. *Punch,* 8 (14 June): 262.
(Spielmann, p. 323)

396. Signed illustration to "Debate on the Navy." *Punch,* 8 (21 June): 266.
(Spielmann, p. 323)

397. "Letters from a Club Arm-Chair." Signed "Squab." *The Calcutta Star,* 21 June.
(Summerfield, p. 43)

398. "The Ascot Cup Day." [A drawing, with letterpress.] *Punch,* 9 (28 June): 3.
(Spielmann, p. 323)

399. "Stiggins in New Zealand." *Punch,* 9 (28 June): 3. (Spielmann, p. 323)

400. "A Legend of the Rhine [Chaps. III-VI]." [With four illustrations by Cruikshank.] *George Cruikshank's Table-Book,* No. 7 (July): 144-52.

401. "The Chest of Cigars. By Lancelot Wagstaff." *The New Monthly Magazine,* 74 (July): 381-85.

402. "Immense Opportunity." *Punch,* 9 (5 July): 14. (Spielmann, p. 324)

403. "'Appeal to Rome!'" *Punch,* 9 (5 July): 15. (Spielmann, p. 324)

404. "Where are the Hackney-Coaches Gone to?" *Punch,* 9 (5 July): 15.
(Spielmann, p. 324)

405. "Most Noble Festivities." [With an illustration probably not by Thackeray.] *Punch,* 9 (5 July): 16.
(Spielmann, p. 324)

406. "The Eureka." *Punch,* 9 (5 July): 20.
(Spielmann, p. 324)

407. "The Abdication of Don Carlos." Signed "Launcelot Greaves." [With two illustrations probably not by Thackeray.] *Punch,* 9 (12 July): 24-25.
(Spielmann, p. 324)

408. "British Honour." *Punch,* 9 (12 July): 26.
(Spielmann, p. 324)

409. "Tremendous Sufferings of the Household Brigade." *Punch*, 9 (12 July): 32.   (Spielmann, p. 324)

410. "Reasons Why I Shall Not Send My Son, Gustavus Frederic, to Trinity College, Cambridge." *Punch*, 9 (19 July): 35.
                                                                 (Spielmann, p. 324)

411. "Military Intelligence." *Punch*, 9 (19 July): 40. (Spielmann, p. 324)

412. Signed illustration to "The Gomersal Museum." *Punch*, 9 (19 July): 41.

413. "Soldiering." *Punch*, 9 (26 July): 49.   (Spielmann, p. 324)

414. "Bob Robinson's First Love. By Lancelot Wagstaff, Esq." *The New Monthly Magazine*, 74 (Aug.): 519-25.

415. "A Legend of the Rhine [Chaps. VII-VIII]." [With two illustrations by Cruikshank.] *George Cruikshank's Table-Book*, No. 8 (Aug.): 167-75.

416. "Scholastic." *Punch*, 9 (2 Aug.): 53.   (Spielmann, p. 324)

417. "A House at the West End." Signed "Wilhelmina Amelia Skeggs." *Punch*, 9 (2 Aug.): 55.   (Spielmann, p. 324)

418. Signed illustration to "The Lowly Bard to His Lady Love." *Punch*, 9 (2 Aug.): 56.

419. "A Lucky Speculator." [With an illustration by John Leech.] *Punch*, 9 (2 Aug.): 59.

420. "Jeames of Buckley Square. A Heligy." *Punch*, 9 (2 Aug.): 59.
                                                                 (*Miscellanies*)

421. "War between the Press and the Bar." *Punch*, 9 (9 Aug.): 64-65.
                                                                 (Spielmann, p. 324)

422. "The Pimlico Pavilion. By the Mulligan (of Kilballymulligan)." *Punch*, 9 (9 Aug.): 66.

423. "A Letter from 'Jeames of Buckley Square.'" Signed "Fitz-James de la Pluche." *Punch*, 9 (16 Aug.): 76.

424. "Letters from a Club Arm-Chair." Signed "Squab." *The Calcutta Star*, 21 Aug.   (Summerfield, p. 43)

425. "Punch's Regency." [With an illustration probably not by Thackeray.] *Punch*, 9 (23 Aug.): 94.   (Spielmann, p. 324)

426. "The Stags. A Drama of To-day." [A drawing, with letterpress.] *Punch*, 9 (30 Aug.): 104. (Spielmann, p. 324)

427. "Bar Touting." *Punch*, 9 (30 Aug.): 104. (Spielmann, p. 324)

428. "A Legend of the Rhine [Chaps. IX-X]." [With an illustration by Cruikshank.] *George Cruikshank's Table-Book*, No. 9 (Sept.): 193-200.

429. "Serenade." *Punch*, 9 (6 Sept.): 106. (Spielmann, p. 324)

430. "New Version of God Save the Queen." *Punch*, 9 (6 Sept.): 107. (Spielmann, p. 324)

431. "Interesting Relic at Rosenau." *Punch*, 9 (6 Sept.): 113. (Spielmann, p. 324)

432. "Oysters in Your Own Basins." *Punch*, 9 (6 Sept.): 114. (Spielmann, p. 324)

433. "Meditations on Solitude. By Our Stout Commissioner." With an illustration. *Punch*, 9 (13 Sept.): 123.

434. "Sonnick Sejested by Prince Halbert Gratiously Killing the Staggs at Sacks-Cobug-Gothy." *Punch*, 9 (20 Sept.): 133. (Spielmann, p. 324)

435. "Beulah Spa. By 'Punch's' Commissioner." With two illustrations. *Punch*, 9 (27 Sept.): 137-38.

436. "A Legend of the Rhine [Chap. XI]." [With two illustrations by Cruikshank.] *George Cruikshank's Table-Book*, No. 10 (Oct.): 224-28.

437. *"Dashes at Life with a Free Pencil. By N. P. F. Willis." The Edinburgh Review*, 82 (Oct.): 470-80.

438. "A Seasonable Word on Railways. By Mr. Punch." [With an illustration probably not by Thackeray.] *Punch*, 9 (4 Oct.): 149. (Spielmann, p. 324)

439. "Brighton. By 'Punch's' Commissioner." With three illustrations. *Punch*, 9 (11 Oct.): 158.

440. "The Georges." *Punch*, 9 (11 October): 159.

441. "Dangerous Passage." *Punch*, 9 (11 Oct.): 163. (Spielmann, p. 324)

442. "A Brighton Night Entertainment. By 'Punch's' Commissioner." With four illustrations. *Punch*, 9 (18 Oct.): 168.

443. "Meditations over Brighton. By 'Punch's' Commissioner." With an illustration. *Punch*, 9 (25 Oct.): 187.

444. "A Legend of the Rhine [Chap. XII]." [With an illustration by Cruikshank.] *George Cruikshank's Table-Book*, No. 11 (Nov.): 241-45.

445. "Barmecide Banquets, with Joseph Bregion and Anne Miller. George Savage Fitz-Boodle, Esquire, to the Rev. Lionel Gaster." *Fraser's Magazine*, 32 (Nov.): 584-93.

446. "A Doe in the City." Signed "Frederick Haltamont de Montmorency." With a signed illustration. *Punch*, 9 (1 Nov.): 191.

447. "Jeames on Time Bargings." With an illustration. *Punch*, 9 (1 Nov.): 195.

448. "Jeames's Diary." With an illustration. *Punch*, 9 (8 Nov.): 207-208.

449. "Jeames's Diary." With a signed illustration. *Punch*, 9 (15 Nov.): 210.

450. "Punch's Tribute to O'Connell." With an illustration. *Punch*, 9 (15 Nov.): 215.   (Spielmann, p. 325)

451. "Jeames's Diary." With two illustrations, one signed. *Punch*, 9 (22 Nov.): 227.

452. "Jeames's Diary." With two signed illustrations. *Punch*, 9 (29 Nov.): 233.

453. "Miss Malony and Father Luke." Signed "Biddy Malony." With an illustration. *Punch*, 9 (29 Nov.): 237.   (Spielmann, p. 325)

454. "A Legend of the Rhine [Chap. XIII]." [With an illustration by Cruikshank.] *George Cruikshank's Table-Book*, No. 12 (Dec.): 267-70.

455. "About a Christmas Book. In a Letter from Michael Angelo Titmarsh to Oliver Yorke, Esq." *Fraser's Magazine*, 32 (Dec.): 744-48.

456. "Jeames's Diary." With two signed illustrations. *Punch*, 9 (6 Dec.): 242-43.

457. "Jeames's Diary." With two signed illustrations. *Punch*, 9 (13 Dec.): 251.

458. "John Jones's Remonstrance About the Buckingham Business." [With an illustration probably not by Thackeray.] *Punch*, 9 (20 Dec.): 261.   (Spielmann, p. 325)

459. "The Old Duke." With an illustration. *Punch*, 9 (20 Dec.): 263.
                                              (Spielmann, p. 325)

460. ["Christmas Books.—No. 1." *The Morning Chronicle*, 25 Dec., pp. 5-6.]   ("Chronicle")

461. ["Christmas Books.—No. 2." *The Morning Chronicle*, 26 Dec., p. 5.]   ("Chronicle")

462. "Jeames's Diary." With two signed illustrations. *Punch*, 10 (27 Dec.): 10-11.

463. ["Christmas Books.—No. III." *The Morning Chronicle*, 31 Dec., p. 5.]   ("Chronicle")

1846

464. "Ronsard to His Mistress." Signed "Michael Angelo Titmarsh." *Fraser's Magazine*, 33 (Jan.): 120.

465. "Jeames's Diary." With two illustrations, one signed. *Punch*, 10 (3 Jan.): 13.

466. "Extract of a Letter on the Late Crisis." Signed "T. B. MacPunch." [With an illustration probably not by Thackeray.] *Punch*, 10 (10 Jan.): 23.   (Spielmann, p. 325)

467. "Jeames's Diary." With two illustrations. *Punch*, 10 (10 Jan.): 30-31.

468. "Jeames's Diary." With two illustrations. *Punch*, 10 (17 Jan.): 35.

469. Signed illustration to "The Two Incapables." *Punch*, 10 (17 Jan.): 41.

470. "Jeames's Diary." With an illustration. *Punch*, 10 (31 Jan.): 54-55.

471. "Promotion for Brougham." *Punch*, 10 (31 Jan.): 61.
                                                    (Spielmann, p. 325)

472. "Jeames's Diary." With a signed illustration. *Punch*, 10 (7 Feb.): 72-73.

473. "The Snobs of England. By One of Themselves. Prefatory Remarks." With two illustrations, one signed. *Punch*, 10 (28 Feb.): 101.

474. "A Brother of the Press on the History of a Literary Man, Laman Blanchard, and the Chances of the Literary Profession. In a Letter to the Reverend Francis Sylvester at Rome, from Michael Angelo Titmarsh, Esq." *Fraser's Magazine*, 33 (Mar.): 332-42.

475. "The Snobs of England. By One of Themselves. Chapter I.—The Snob Socially Considered." With an illustration. *Punch*, 10 (7 Mar.): 111-12.

476. "The Snobs of England. By One of Themselves. Chap. II.—The Snob Royal." With an illustration. *Punch*, 10 (14 Mar.): 115.

477. "Titmarsh *v.* Tait." Signed "Michael-Angelo Titmarsh." With an illustration. *Punch*, 10 (14 Mar.): 124.

478. ["Carus's *Travels in England.*" *The Morning Chronicle*, 16 Mar., p. 5.]
("Chronicle")

479. "The Snobs of England. By One of Themselves. Chapter III.—The Influence of the Aristocracy on Snobs." With two illustrations. *Punch*, 10 (21 Mar.): 125-26.

480. "[Burton's] *Life and Correspondence of David Hume.*" *The Morning Chronicle*, 23 Mar., p. 6. (*Letters*, 2: 234)

481. "The Snobs of England. By One of Themselves. Chapter IV. 'The Court Circular,' and Its Influence on Snobs." With two illustrations. *Punch*, 10 (28 Mar.): 137-38.

482. Signed illustration to "Naval Operations." *Punch*, 10 (28 Mar.): 145.

483. "On Some Illustrated Children's Books. By Michael Angelo Titmarsh." *Fraser's Magazine*, 33 (Apr.): 495-502.

484. "The Snobs of England. By One of Themselves. Chap. V.—What Snobs Admire." With two illustrations, one signed. *Punch*, 10 (4 Apr.): 147.

485. ["*Travels in the Punjab.* By Mohan Lal, Esq." *The Morning Chronicle*, 6 Apr., p. 6.]
("Chronicle")

486. ["*The Novitiate; or, a Year among the English Jesuits.* By Andrew Steinmetz." *The Morning Chronicle*, 11 Apr., p. 5.]
("Chronicle")

487. "The Snobs of England. By One of Themselves. Chapter VI.—On Some Respectable Snobs." With an illustration. *Punch*, 10 (11 Apr.): 157-58.

488. "The Snobs of England. By One of Themselves. Chap. VII.—On Some Respectable Snobs." With a signed illustration. *Punch*, 10 (18 Apr.): 167.

489. "The Irish Curfew Bill." *Punch*, 10 (18 Apr.): 174. (Spielmann, p. 326)

490. ["(Bulwer-Lytton's) *The New Timon.*" *The Morning Chronicle*, 21 Apr., p. 5.] ("Chronicle")

491. "The Snobs of England. By One of Themselves. Chapter VIII.— Great City Snobs." With two illustrations, one signed. *Punch*, 10 (25 Apr.): 177-78.

492. ["The Exhibitions of the Societies of Water Colour Painters." *The Morning Chronicle*, 27 Apr., p. 5.] ("Chronicle")

493. "The Snobs of England. By One of Themselves. Chap. IX.—On Some Military Snobs." With an illustration. *Punch*, 10 (2 May): 197.

494. [*Sketches of English Character.* By Mrs. Gore." *The Morning Chronicle*, 4 May, p. 5.] ("Chronicle")

495. ["The Exhibition of the Royal Academy." *The Morning Chronicle*, 5 May, p. 6.] ("Chronicle")

496. ["The Exhibition of the Royal Academy. (Second Notice.)" *The Morning Chronicle*, 7 May, p. 5.] ("Chronicle")

497. "The Snobs of England. By One of Themselves. Chapter X.— Military Snobs." With two illustrations. *Punch*, 10 (9 May): 207.

498. "Royal Academy." Signed "Modest Merit." With six illustrations, two signed. *Punch*, 10 (9 May): 214. (Spielmann, p. 326)

499. ["Royal Academy. (Third Notice.)" *The Morning Chronicle*, 11 May, p. 5.] ("Chronicle")

500. "The Snobs of England. By One of Themselves. Chap. XI.—On Clerical Snobs." With an illustration. *Punch*, 10 (16 May): 217.

501. "Jeames on the Gauge Question." With an illustration. *Punch*, 10 (16 May): 223.

502. "The Snobs of England. By One of Themselves. Chapter XII.—On Clerical Snobs and Snobbishness." With an illustration. *Punch*, 10 (23 May): 227-28.

503. "The Snobs of England. By One of Themselves. Chap. XIII.—On Clerical Snobs." With an illustration accompanied by letterpress. *Punch*, 10 (30 May): 238-39.

504. "The Snobs of England. By One of Themselves. Chapter XIV.—On University Snobs." With two signed illustrations. *Punch*, 10 (6 June): 250-51.

505. "The Snobs of England. By One of Themselves. Chap. XV.—On University Snobs." With a signed illustration. *Punch*, 10 (13 June): 261.

506. "Mr. Jeames Again." With a signed illustration. *Punch*, 10 (13 June): 267.

507. ["Haydon's *Lectures on Painting and Design.*" *The Morning Chronicle*, 19 June, p. 6.] ("Chronicle")

508. "The Snobs of England. By One of Themselves. Chapter XVI.—On Literary Snobs." With two illustrations, one signed. *Punch*, 10 (20 June): 271.

509. "The Snobs of England. By One of Themselves. Chap. XVII.—On Literary Snobs. In a Letter from 'One of Themselves' to Mr. Smith, the celebrated Penny-a-Liner." [With an illustration probably not by Thackeray.] *Punch*, 10 (27 June): 281.

510. ["Alexis Soyer, *The Gastronomic Regenerator.*" *The Morning Chronicle*, 4 July, p. 5.] ("Chronicle")

511. "A New Naval Drama." With two illustrations, one signed. *Punch*, 11 (4 July): 2. (Spielmann, p. 326)

512. "The Snobs of England. By One of Themselves. Chapter XVIII.—On Some Political Snobs." *Punch*, 11 (4 July): 4.

513. "Black Monday." *Punch*, 11 (4 July): 12. (Spielmann, p. 326)

514. "Signs of the Times." *Punch*, 11 (4 July): 12. (Spielmann, p. 326)

515. "The Snobs of England. By One of Themselves. Chap. XIX.—On Whig Snobs." With two illustrations, one signed. *Punch*, 11 (11 July): 19.

516. "The Snobs of England. By One of Themselves. Chapter XX. On Conservative or Country-Party Snobs." With two illustrations. *Punch*, 11 (18 July): 23.

517. "The Snobs of England. By One of Themselves. Chap. XXI.—Are There Any Whig Snobs?" With an illustration. *Punch*, 11 (25 July): 39.

518. "Proposals for a Continuation of Ivanhoe. In a Letter to Monsieur Alexandre Dumas, by Monsieur Michael Angelo Titmarsh. [Vol. I]." *Fraser's Magazine*, 34 (Aug.): 237-45.

519. "The Snobs of England. By One of Themselves. Chapter XXII.—On the Snob Civilian." *Punch*, 11 (1 Aug.): 43.

520. "One 'Who can Administer to a Mind Diseased.'" [A signed drawing, with letterpress.] *Punch*, 11 (1 Aug.): 50. (Spielmann, p. 327)

521. "May Difference of Opinion Never Alter Friendship!" [A drawing, with letterpress.] *Punch*, 11 (1 Aug.): 52. (Spielmann, p. 327)

522. "The Snobs of England. By One of Themselves. Chap. XXIII.—On Radical Snobs." With an illustration. *Punch*, 11 (8 Aug.): 59.

523. Signed illustration to "White-bait Dinner to Sir Robert Peel." *Punch*, 11 (8 Aug.): 61.

524. "A Tea-Table Tragedy." [A signed drawing, with letterpress.] *Punch*, 11 (15 Aug.): 63.

525. "The Snobs of England. By One of Themselves. Chapter XXIV.—A Little More About Irish Snobs." *Punch*, 11 (15 Aug.): 63.

526. "The Meeting between the Sultan and Mehemet Ali." With an illustration. *Punch*, 11 (15 Aug.): 72. (Spielmann, p. 327)

527. "The Heavies. Captain Ragg and Cornet Famish." [A drawing, with letterpress.] *Punch*, 11 (15 Aug.): 72. (Spielmann, p. 327)

528. ["Moore's *History of Ireland; from the earliest Kings of that Realm down to its last Chief.*" *The Morning Chronicle*, 20 Aug., p. 5.] ("Chronicle")

529. "The Snobs of England. By One of Themselves. Chapter XXV.—Party-Giving Snobs." With a signed illustration. *Punch*, 11 (22 Aug.): 81-82.

530. "The Speaking Machine." [With an illustration probably not by Thackeray.] *Punch*, 11 (22 Aug.): 83. (Spielmann, p. 327)

531. ["Cooper's *Ravensnest; or the Red Skins.* By the Author of 'The Pilot,' &c." *The Morning Chronicle*, 27 Aug., p. 6.] ("Chronicle")

532. "The Snobs of England. By One of Themselves. Chapter XXVI.—Dining-out Snobs." With a signed illustration. *Punch*, 11 (29 Aug.): 91-92.

533. "Half an Hour Before Dinner. Niminy and Piminy Staring at the Ladies Seated in a Circle in the Drawing-room." [A signed drawing, with letterpress.] *Punch*, 11 (29 Aug.): 92.

534. "Proposals for a Continuation of Ivanhoe. In a Letter to Monsieur Alexandre Dumas, by Monsieur Michael Angelo Titmarsh. Vols. II. and III." *Fraser's Magazine*, 34 (Sept.): 359-67.

535. ["Lane's *Life at the Water Cure.*" *The Morning Chronicle*, 1 Sept., p. 5.]
("Chronicle")

536. "The Snobs of England. By One of Themselves. Chapter XXVII.— Dinner-Giving Snobs Further Considered." With two illustrations, one signed. *Punch*, 11 (5 Sept.): 95-96.

537. "The Heavies. Captain Rag Dictating to Cornet Famish." [A drawing, with letterpress.] *Punch*, 11 (5 Sept.): 103. (Spielmann, p. 327)

538. "The Snobs of England. By One of Themselves. Chapter XXVIII.— Some Continental Snobs." With an illustration. *Punch*, 11 (12 Sept.): 105-106.

539. "The Snobs of England. By One of Themselves. Chapter XXIX.— Continental Snobbery Continued." With three illustrations. *Punch*, 11 (19 Sept.): 115.

540. "What's Come to the Clubs?" Signed "Alured Mogyns de Mogyns." With three illustrations. *Punch*, 11 (19 Sept.): 123.
(Spielmann, p. 327)

541. "*The Poetical Works of Horace Smith.*" *The Morning Chronicle*, 21 Sept., p. 6.
(*Letters*, 2: 249)

542. ["*Diary and Letters of Madame d'Arblay.*" *The Morning Chronicle*, 25 Sept., p. 6.]
("Chronicle")

543. "The Snobs of England. By One of Themselves. Chapter XXX.— English Snobs on the Continent." With an illustration. *Punch*, 11 (26 Sept.): 125.

544. Signed illustration to "Matrimonial Dictionary." *Punch*, 11 (26 Sept.): 135.

545. "The Snobs of England. By One of Themselves. Chapter XXXI.— On Some Country Snobs." With a signed illustration. *Punch*, 11 (3 Oct.): 141.

546. ["*Royal Palaces.* F. W. Trench." *The Morning Chronicle*, 5 Oct., p. 5.]
("Chronicle")

547. "The Snobs of England. By One of Themselves. Chapter XXXII.— A Visit to Some Country Snobs." With a signed illustration. *Punch*, 11 (10 Oct.): 148-49.

548. "The Snobs of England. By One of Themselves. Chapter XXXIII.
—On Some Country Snobs." With three illustrations, one signed.
Punch, 11 (17 Oct.): 157-58.

549. "The Snobs of England. By One of Themselves. Chapter XXXIV.—
A Visit to Some Country Snobs." With an illustration. *Punch*, 11
(24 Oct.): 167.

550. Signed illustration to "A Perilous Precedent." *Punch*, 11 (24 Oct.):
169.

551. "The Household Brigade." With three illustrations. *Punch*, 11
(24 Oct.): 174.   (Spielmann, p. 328)

552. "The Snobs of England. By One of Themselves. Chapter XXXV.—
On Some Country Snobs." With an illustration. *Punch*, 11
(31 Oct.): 177-78.

553. "A Scene in St. James's Park." [A signed drawing.] *Punch*, 11
(31 Oct.): 180.

554. "The Snobs of England. By One of Themselves. Chapter XXXVI.—
A Visit to Some Country Snobs." With a signed illustration. *Punch*,
11 (7 Nov.): 187.

555. Signed illustration to "Tales for the Marines. Tale the Eighth."
Punch, 11 (7 Nov.): 189.

556. Signed illustration to "Treatment of Pictures in the National Gallery." *Punch*, 11 (7 Nov.): 193.

557. "The Snobs of England. By One of Themselves. Chapter XXXVII.
—On Some Country Snobs." With two illustrations, one signed.
Punch, 11 (14 Nov.): 197.

558. Signed illustration to "Good News for Anglers." *Punch*, 11
(21 Nov.): 209.

559. "The Snobs of England. By One of Themselves. Chapter XXXVIII.
—A Visit to Some Country Snobs." With an illustration. *Punch*, 11
(21 Nov.): 215.

560. Signed illustration to "The Court Apollo." *Punch*, 11 (28 Nov.):
220.

561. "Kitchen Melodies.—Curry." With an illustration. *Punch*, 11
(28 Nov.): 221.   (Spielmann, p. 328)

562. "The Snobs of England. By One of Themselves. Chapter XXXIX.
—Snobbium Gatherum." With a signed illustration. *Punch*, 11 (28 Nov.): 225-26.

563. "The Snobs of England. By One of Themselves. Chapter XL.—Snobs and Marriage." With two illustrations. *Punch*, 11 (5 Dec.): 229.

564. "The Snobs of England. By One of Themselves. Chapter XLI.—Snobs and Marriage." *Punch*, 11 (12 Dec.): 247-48.

565. "The Snobs of England. By One of Themselves. Chapter XLII.—Snobs and Marriage." With an illustration. *Punch*, 11 (19 Dec.): 251-52.

566. "The Snobs of England. By One of Themselves. Chapter XLIII.—Snobs and Marriage." With a signed illustration. *Punch*, 11 (26 Dec.): 261-62.

567. Signed illustration to "Music in Ebony." *Punch*, 11 (26 Dec.): 263.

568. "An Eastern Adventure of the Fat Contributor." [With an illustration by John Leech.] *Punch's Pocket Book for 1847*. London: Punch, [1846], pp. 148-56.

1847

569. "Vanity Fair. Pen and Pencil Sketches of English Society. No. 1 [Chaps. I-IV]." With an illustrated title page and fourteen other illustrations. (Jan.), pp. 1-32.

570. "A Grumble About The Christmas Books. By Michael Angelo Titmarsh." *Fraser's Magazine*, 35 (Jan.): 111-26.

571. "The Snobs of England. By One of Themselves. Chapter XLIV.—Club Snobs." With two illustrations, one signed. *Punch*, 12 (2 Jan.): 7-8.

572. "The Snobs of England. By One of Themselves. Chapter XLV.—Club Snobs." With three illustrations. *Punch*, 12 (9 Jan.): 11-12.

573. "The Mahogany Tree." [With an illustration by Richard Doyle.] *Punch*, 12 (9 Jan.): 13.

574. "The Snobs of England. By One of Themselves. Chapter XLVI.—Club Snobs." With two illustrations. *Punch*, 12 (16 Jan.): 23-24.

575. Signed illustration to "Piratical Expeditions." *Punch*, 12 (23 Jan.): 34.

576. "The Snobs of England. By One of Themselves. Chapter XLVII. Club Snobs." With an illustration. *Punch*, 12 (23 Jan.): 34-35.

577. "The Snobs of England. By One of Themselves. Chapter XLVIII.— Club Snobs." With three illustrations. *Punch*, 12 (30 Jan.): 43-44.

578. Signed illustration to "The Value of Health at Liverpool." *Punch*, 12 (30 Jan.): 44.

579. Signed illustration to "New Grand Junction Line." *Punch*, 12 (30 Jan.): 46.

580. "Vanity Fair. Pen and Pencil Sketches of English Society. No. 2 [Chaps. V-VII]." With an illustrated title page and seventeen other illustrations. (Feb.), pp. 33-64.

581. "The Snobs of England. By One of Themselves. Chapter XLIX.— Club Snobs." With a signed illustration. *Punch*, 12 (6 Feb.): 53.

582. "Horrid Tragedy in Private Life!" [A signed drawing.] *Punch*, 12 (6 Feb.): 59.

583. Two illustrations, one signed, to "Union is Strength." *Punch*, 12 (6 Feb.): 61.

584. "The Snobs of England. By One of Themselves. Chapter L.—Club Snobs." With an illustration. *Punch*, 12 (13 Feb.): 72-73.

585. "The Snobs of England. By One of Themselves. Chapter LI.—Club Snobs." With two signed illustrations. *Punch*, 12 (20 Feb.): 81-82.

586. "The Snobs of England. By One of Themselves. Chapter Last." With an illustration. *Punch*, 12 (27 Feb.): 85-86.

587. "Vanity Fair. Pen and Pencil Sketches of English Society. No. 3 [Chaps. VIII-XI]." With an illustrated title page and ten other illustrations. (Mar.), pp. 65-96.

588. "Love Songs Made Easy. What Makes My Heart to Thrill and Glow? Song by Fitzroy Clarence." With an Introduction and an illustration. *Punch*, 12 (6 Mar.): 101.

589. "Mr. Jeames's Sentiments on the Cambridge Election." Signed "Jeames de la Pluche." *Punch*, 12 (6 Mar.): 102.

590. Signed illustration to "'The Least Said, the Soonest Mended.'" *Punch*, 12 (6 Mar.): 104.

591. "The Cambridge Address to Prince Albert." With an illustration. *Punch*, 12 (13 Mar.): 106.   (Spielmann, p. 329)

592. "Literature at a Stand." [A signed drawing, with letterpress.] *Punch*, 12 (13 Mar.): 113.

593. Signed illustration to "Revolution at Munich.—Beauty's Bull-dog." *Punch*, 12 (13 Mar.): 114.

594. "Love Songs by the Fat Contributor. The Domestic Love Song. Ye Cane-bottomed Chair." With an Introduction and two illustrations. *Punch*, 12 (27 Mar.): 125.

595. "Vanity Fair. Pen and Pencil Sketches of English Society. No. 4 [Chaps. XII-XIV]." With an illustrated title page and ten other illustrations. (Apr.), pp. 97-128.

596. "Punch's Prize Novelists. [With an Introduction.] George de Barnwell. [By] E. L. B. L. B. B. L. L. B. B. B. L. L. L." With a signed illustration. *Punch*, 12 (3 Apr.): 136-37.

597. "Punch's Prize Novelists. George de Barnwell.—Vol. II. By Sir E. L. B. L. B. B. L. L. B. B. B. L. L. L." With a signed illustration. *Punch*, 12 (10 Apr.): 146-47.

598. "Punch's Prize Novelists. George de Barnwell.—Vol. III. By Sir E. L. B. L. B. B. L. L. B. B. B. L. L. L." With a signed illustration. *Punch*, 12 (17 Apr.): 155.

599. "Punch's Prize Novelists. Codlingsby. By B. de Shrewsbury, Esq." With an illustration. *Punch*, 12 (24 Apr.): 166.

600. Signed illustration to "Peter the Putter-Down Preacheth a Newe Crusade." *Punch*, 12 (24 Apr.): 173.

601. "Vanity Fair. Pen and Pencil Sketches of English Society. No. 5 [Chaps. XV-XVIII]." With an illustrated title page and nine other illustrations. (May), pp. 129-60.

602. Signed illustration to "English Tendencies." *Punch*, 12 (1 May): 186.

603. "Punch's Prize Novelists. Codlingsby. By B. de Shrewsbury." With an illustration. *Punch*, 12 (15 May): 198-99.

604. "A Disputed Genealogy." Signed "Brian Tuggles Tuggles." *Punch*, 12 (15 May): 204-205.   (Spielmann, p. 329)

605. "Punch's Prize Novelists. Codlingsby." With an illustration. *Punch*, 12 (22 May): 213-14.

606. "Punch's Prize Novelists. Codlingsby. By B. de Shrewsbury." With an illustration. *Punch*, 12 (29 May): 223.

607. "Vanity Fair. Pen and Pencil Sketches of English Society. No. 6 [Chaps. XIX-XXII]." With an illustrated title page and nine other illustrations. (June), pp. 161-92.

608. "Love-Songs of the Fat Contributor. The Ghazul, or Oriental Love-Song. The Rocks. The Merry Bard. The Caique." With two illustrations. *Punch*, 12 (5 June): 227.

609. "Punch's Prize Novelists. Lords and Liveries. By the Authoress of 'Dukes and Dejeuners,' 'Hearts and Diamonds,' 'Marchionesses and Milliners,' etc., etc." With two illustrations. *Punch*, 12 (12 June): 237-38.

610. Signed illustration to "The Thames Derby." *Punch*, 12 (12 June): 240.

611. "Punch's Prize Novelists. Lords and Liveries. By the Authoress of 'Dukes and Dejeuners,' 'Hearts and Diamonds,' 'Marchionesses and Milliners,' etc., etc." With an illustration. *Punch*, 12 (19 June): 247.

612. "Punch's Prize Novelists. Lords and Liveries. By the Authoress of 'Dukes and Dejeuners,' 'Hearts and Diamonds,' 'Marchionesses and Milliners,' etc., etc." With an illustration. *Punch*, 12 (26 June): 257-58.

613. "Vanity Fair. Pen and Pencil Sketches of English Society. No. 7 [Chaps. XXIII-XXV]." With an illustrated title page and nine other illustrations. (July), pp. 193-224.

614. "Punch's Prize Novelists. Barbazure. By G. P. R. Jeames, Esq., etc." With an illustration. *Punch*, 13 (10 July): 2.

615. "Professor Byles's Opinion of the Westminster Hall Exhibition." Signed "Growley Byles." With six illustrations. *Punch*, 13 (10 July): 8-9.   (Spielmann, p. 330)

616. "Punch's Prize Novelists. Barbazure. By G. P. R. Jeames, Esq., etc." With two illustrations. *Punch*, 13 (17 July): 12-13.

617. "Punch's Prize Novelists. Barbazure. By G. P. R. Jeames, Esq., etc." With two illustrations. *Punch*, 13 (24 July): 21-22.

618. "Vanity Fair. Pen and Pencil Sketches of English Society. No. 8 [Chaps. XXVI-XXIX]." With an illustrated title page and eleven other illustrations. (Aug.), pp. 225-56.

619. Signed illustration to "The Finsbury Letters. Out-of-Town Friends." *Punch*, 13 (7 Aug.): 42.

620. Signed illustration to "A Song for Sibthorp." *Punch*, 13 (7 Aug.): 47.

621. "Punch's Prize Novelists. Phil. Fogarty—A Tale of the Fighting Onety-Oneth. By Harry Rollicker." With an illustration. *Punch*, 13 (7 Aug.): 49-50.

622. Signed illustration to "The House of Shakspeare and The House of Coburg." *Punch*, 13 (14 Aug.): 52.

623. "Punch's Prize Novelists. Phil. Fogarty—A Tale of the Fighting Onety-Oneth. By Harry Rollicker." With two illustrations, one signed. *Punch*, 13 (14 Aug.): 56-57.

624. Signed illustration to "Petty Bribery and Corruption." *Punch*, 13 (21 Aug.): 61.

625. "Punch's Prize Novelists. Phil. Fogarty—A Tale of the Fighting Onety-Oneth. By Harry Rollicker." With two illustrations. *Punch*, 13 (21 Aug.): 67-68.

626. "Punch's Prize Novelists. Crinoline. By Je-mes Pl-sh, Esq." With two illustrations. *Punch*, 13 (28 Aug.): 72-73.

627. "Vanity Fair. Pen and Pencil Sketches of English Society. No. 9 [Chaps. XXX-XXXII]." With an illustrated title page and nine other illustrations. (Sept.), pp. 257-88.

628. "Punch's Prize Novelists. Crinoline. By Je-mes Pl-sh, Esq." With two illustrations. *Punch*, 13 (4 Sept.): 82-83.

629. "Punch's Prize Novelists. Crinoline. By Je-mes Pl-sh, Esq. Chap. III.—The Castle of the Island of Fogo." With two illustrations, one signed. *Punch*, 13 (11 Sept.): 97-98.

630. "Punch to the Queen of Spain." [With an illustration by Richard Doyle.] *Punch*, 13 (18 Sept.): 101.   (Spielmann, p. 330)

631. "Punch's Prize Novelists. The Stars and Stripes. By the Author of 'The Last of the Mulligans,' 'Pilot,' &c." With an illustration. *Punch*, 13 (25 Sept.): 117-18.

632. "Vanity Fair. Pen and Pencil Sketches of English Society. No. 10 [Chaps. XXXIII-XXXV]." With an illustrated title page and seven other illustrations. (Oct.), pp. 289-320.

633. "Punch's Prize Novelists. The Stars and Stripes. By the Author of 'The Last of the Mulligans,' 'Pilot,' &c." With an illustration. *Punch*, 13 (9 Oct.): 137.

634. Signed illustration to "Young Israel to Punch." *Punch*, 13 (9 Oct.): 140.

635. "Signs of a Move." *Punch*, 13 (16 Oct.): 143. (Spielmann, p. 330)

636. "X. Y. Z." [With an illustration by Richard Doyle.] *Punch*, 13 (16 Oct.): 147. (Spielmann, p. 330)

637. "Caution to Tradesmen." *Punch*, 13 (16 Oct.): 150.
(Spielmann, p. 330)

638. "Brighton in 1847. By the F. C." With an illustration. *Punch*, 13 (23 Oct.): 153.

639. "Brighton in 1847. By the F. C." With two illustrations. *Punch*, 13 (30 Oct.): 167-68.

640. "Oxford Public Oratory." *Punch*, 13 (30 Oct.): 170.
(Spielmann, p. 330)

641. "Vanity Fair. Pen and Pencil Sketches of English Society. No. 11 [Chaps. XXXVI-XXXVIII]." With an illustrated title page and ten other illustrations. (Nov.), pp. 321-52.

642. "The New Peers Spiritual." *Punch*, 13 (6 Nov.): 172.
(Spielmann, p. 330)

643. "Latest from Mexico." *Punch*, 13 (6 Nov.): 179. (Spielmann, p. 330)

644. "Travels in London." Signed "Spec." With an illustration. *Punch*, 13 (20 Nov.): 193.

645. "Travels in London. The Curate's Walk." Signed "Spec." With two illustrations. *Punch*, 13 (27 Nov.); 201-202.

646. "Vanity Fair. Pen and Pencil Sketches of English Society. No. 12 [Chaps. XXXIX-XLII]." With an illustrated title page and nine other illustrations. (Dec.), pp. 353-84.

647. "Travels in London. A Walk with the Curate." Signed "Spec." With two illustrations. *Punch*, 13 (4 Dec.): 211-12.

648. "Travels in London. A Dinner in the City." Signed "Spec." With two illustrations. *Punch*, 13 (11 Dec.): 223-224.

649. "Punch and the Influenza." With four illustrations. *Punch*, 13 (18 Dec.): 238.   (Spielmann, p. 330)

650. "Travels in London. A Dinner in the City." Signed "Spec." With two illustrations, one signed. *Punch*, 13 (25 Dec.): 247-48.

651. "The Anglers. By W. M. Thackeray, Esq." With an illustration. In *Fisher's Drawing Room Scrap-Book*, ed. The Hon. Mrs. Norton. (London: Fisher, 1847), pp. 38-39.

1848

652. "Vanity Fair. Pen and Pencil Sketches of English Society. No. 13 [Chaps. XLIII-XLVI]." With an illustrated title page and nine other illustrations. (Jan.), pp. 385-416.

653. "Travels in London. A Dinner in the City." Signed "Spec." With an illustration. *Punch*, 13 (1 Jan.): 251.

654. "Travels in London. A Night's Pleasure." Signed "Spec." With two illustrations. *Punch*, 14 (8 Jan.): 11.

655. "Travels in London. A Night's Pleasure." Signed "Spec." With an illustration. *Punch*, 14 (15 Jan.): 19.

656. "Travels in London. A Night's Pleasure." Signed "Spec." With three illustrations. *Punch*, 14 (22 Jan.): 29-30.

657. "Travels in London. A Night's Pleasure." Signed "Spec." With an illustration. *Punch*, 14 (29 Jan.): 35-36.

658. "Vanity Fair. Pen and Pencil Sketches of English Society. No. 14 [Chaps. XLVII-L]." With an illustrated title page and ten other illustrations. (Feb.), pp. 417-48.

659. "Travels in London. A Night's Pleasure." Signed "Spec." With two illustrations, one signed. *Punch*, 14 (12 Feb.): 61-62.

660. "Travels in London. A Night's Pleasure." Signed "Spec." With an illustration. *Punch*, 14 (19 Feb.): 65-66.

661. "Mr. Punch for Repeal." With two illustrations. *Punch*, 14 (26 Feb.): 81.   (Spielmann, p. 331)

662. "Vanity Fair. Pen and Pencil Sketches of English Society. No. 15 [Chaps. LI-LIII]." With an illustrated title page and eight other illustrations. (Mar.), pp. 449-80.

663. "Travels in London. A Club in an Uproar." Signed "Spec." With two illustrations. *Punch*, 14 (11 Mar.): 95-96.

664. "Heroic Sacrifice." *Punch*, 14 (11 Mar.): 96.   (Spielmann, p. 331)

665. "What Has Happened to the *Morning Chronicle?*" *Punch*, 14 (11 Mar.): 100.   (Spielmann, p. 331)

666. "The Worst Cut of All." *Punch*, 14 (11 Mar.): 100. (Spielmann, p. 331)

667. "Old England for Ever!" *Punch*, 14 (11 Mar.): 105.
                                        (Spielmann, p. 331)

668. "Meeting on Kennington Common." *The Morning Chronicle*, 14 Mar., p. 7.   (*Letters*, 2: 364)

669. "Chartist Meeting." *The Morning Chronicle*, 15 Mar., p. 7.
                                        (*Letters*, 2: 365)

670. "A Dream of the Future." With an illustration. *Punch*, 14 (18 Mar.): 107.   (Spielmann, p. 331)

671. "Travels in London. A Roundabout Ride." Signed "Spec." With an illustration. *Punch*, 14 (25 Mar.): 119.

672. "Mr. Smith and Moses." With an illustration. *Punch*, 14 (25 Mar.): 127.   (Spielmann, p. 331)

673. "The Ex-King at Madame Tussaud's." *Punch*, 14 (25 Mar.): 128.
                                        (Spielmann, p. 331)

674. "Vanity Fair. Pen and Pencil Sketches of English Society. No. 16 [Chaps. LIV-LVI]." With an illustrated title page and nine other illustrations. (Apr.), pp. 481-512.

675. "The Persecution of British Footmen. By Mr. Jeames." With an illustration. *Punch*, 14 (1 Apr.): 131.

676. "The Persecution of British Footmen. By Mr. Jeames." With two illustrations. *Punch*, 14 (8 Apr.): 143-44.

677. "Irish Gems. From the 'Benighted Irishman.'" With an illustration. *Punch*, 14 (15 Apr.): 153.   (Spielmann, p. 331)

678. "French Sympathisers." With an illustration. *Punch*, 14 (22 Apr.): 171.   (Spielmann, p. 331)

679. "An After-Dinner Conversation." *Punch*, 14 (29 Apr.): 182.
     (Spielmann, p. 331)

680. "Vanity Fair. Pen and Pencil Sketches of English Society. No. 17 [Chaps. LVII-LX]." With an illustrated title page and nine other illustrations. (May), pp. 513-44.

681. "The Battle of Limerick." *Punch*, 14 (13 May): 195. (*Miscellanies*)

682. "The Portfolio." With two illustrations. *Punch*, 14 (13 May): 205-206.
     (Spielmann, p. 331)

683. "On the New Forward Movement. A Letter from our old friend, Mr. Snob, to Mr. Joseph Hume." With an illustration. *Punch*, 14 (20 May): 207-208.
     (Spielmann, p. 331)

684. "Mr. Snob's Remonstrance with Mr. Smith." With an illustration. *Punch*, 14 (27 May): 217.
     (Spielmann, p. 331)

685. "A Little Dinner at Timmins's." With three illustrations. *Punch*, 14 (27 May): 219-20, 223.

686. "Vanity Fair. Pen and Pencil Sketches of English Society. No. 18 [Chaps. LXI-LXIII]." With an illustrated title page and eight other illustrations. (June), pp. 545-76.

687. "Yesterday; A Tale of the Polish Ball. By a Lady of Fashion." With an illustration. *Punch*, 14 (10 June): 237.
     (Spielmann, p. 331)

688. "A Little Dinner at Timmins's." With an illustration. *Punch*, 14 (17 June): 247.

689. "A Dilemma." *Punch*, 14 (24 June): 257.
     (Spielmann, p. 331)

690. "A Little Dinner at Timmins's." *Punch*, 14 (24 June): 258.

691. "Vanity Fair. Pen and Pencil Sketches of English Society. Nos. 19-20 [Chaps. LXIV-LXVII]." With an illustrated title page, twelve other illustrations, and an additional illustrated title page for the bound volume. (July), pp. 577-624.

692. Signed illustration to "The Brummagem French Emperor." *Punch*, 15 (1 July): 3.

693. "A Little Dinner at Timmins's." With an illustration. *Punch*, 15 (1 July): 5.

694. "A Little Dinner at Timmins's." With an illustration. *Punch*, 15 (8 July): 13.

695. "The Hampstead Road. A Comedy in Four Tableaux." [Four drawings, with letterpress.] *Punch*, 15 (15 July): 30. (Spielmann, p. 332)

696. "A Little Dinner at Timmins's." With an illustration. *Punch*, 15 (22 July): 33-34.

697. "A Little Dinner at Timmins's." With an illustration. *Punch*, 15 (29 July): 43.

698. Signed illustration to "The Model Mother." *Punch*, 15 (29 July): 51.

699. "Military Correspondence." With six illustrations. *Punch*, 15 (5 Aug.): 62-63. (Spielmann, p. 332)

700. "Latest from the Continent." With an illustration. *Punch*, 15 (26 Aug.): 87. (Spielmann, p. 332)

701. "A Simile." *Punch*, 15 (26 Aug.): 93. (Spielmann, p. 332)

702. "Letters to a Nobleman Visiting Ireland." Signed "Hibernis Hibernior." With an illustration. *Punch*, 15 (2 Sept.): 95-96.
(Spielmann, p. 332)

703. "Authors' Miseries. No. 1." [A drawing, with letterpress.] *Punch*, 15 (2 Sept.): 105.

704. "Letters to a Nobleman Visiting Ireland." Signed "Hibernis Hibernior." With a signed illustration. *Punch*, 15 (9 Sept.): 107.
(Spielmann, p. 332)

705. "Authors' Miseries. No. II." [A drawing, with letterpress.] *Punch*, 15 (9 Sept.): 115.

706. "The Balmoral Gazette." With an illustration. *Punch*, 15 (16 Sept.): 119. (Spielmann, p. 332)

707. "Authors' Miseries. No. III." [A drawing, with letterpress.] *Punch*, 15 (23 Sept.): 127.

708. "Sanitarianism and Insanitarianism." *Punch*, 15 (23 Sept.): 127-28.
(Spielmann, p. 332)

709. "Hemigration made Heasy. To Lord Hashley." Signed "Ninethowsndninunderdannninetynine." *Punch*, 15 (30 Sept.): 143.
(Spielmann, p. 332)

710. "Authors' Miseries. No. IV." [A drawing, with letterpress.] *Punch*, 15 (30 Sept.): 144.

711. "'Is There Anything in the Paper?'" With an illustration. *Punch*, 15 (30 Sept.): 144-45. (Spielmann, p. 332)

712. "Emigration to America." *Punch*, 15 (30 Sept.): 145.
    (Spielmann, p. 332)

713. "Authors' Miseries. No. V." [A drawing, with letterpress.] *Punch*, 15 (7 Oct.): 154.

714. "The History of Pendennis. His Fortunes and Misfortunes, His Friends and His Greatest Enemy. No. 1 [Chaps. I-III]." With an illustrated title page and eight other illustrations. (Nov.), pp. 1-32.

715. "Authors' Miseries. No. VI." [A drawing, with letterpress.] *Punch*, 15 (4 Nov.): 198.

716. "Science at Cambridge." With an illustration. *Punch*, 15 (11 Nov.): 201.
    ("Punch")

717. "A Side-Box Talk." [A signed drawing, with letterpress.] *Punch*, 15 (18 Nov.): 218.

718. "Traitors to the British Government." Signed "Hibernis Hibernior." *Punch*, 15 (18 Nov.): 218-19.
    ("Punch")

719. "A Bow-Street Ballad; By a Gentleman of the Force." Signed "Pleaceman X. 54." With an illustration. *Punch*, 15 (25 Nov.): 229.

720. "The History of Pendennis. His Fortunes and Misfortunes, His Friends and His Greatest Enemy. No. 2 [Chaps. IV-VI]." With an illustrated title page and seven other illustrations. (Dec.), pp. 33-64.

721. "Death of the Earl of Robinson. (In the manner of a popular Necrographer)." With an illustration. *Punch*, 15 (2 Dec.): 231.
    ("Punch")

722. "Authors' Miseries. No. VII." [A drawing, with letterpress.] *Punch*, 15 (2 Dec.): 240.

723. "Bow Street Ballads.—No. II. Jacob Omnium's Hoss. A New Pallice Court Chaunt." With an illustration. *Punch*, 15 (9 Dec.): 251.

724. "The Great Squattleborough *Soirée*." Signed "Leontius Androcles Hugglestone." With a signed illustration. *Punch*, 15 (16 Dec.): 253-54.
    ("Punch")

725. "The Three Christmas Waits." With an illustration. *Punch*, 15 (23 Dec.): 265.
    ("Punch")

1849

726. "The History of Pendennis. His Fortunes and Misfortunes, His Friends and His Greatest Enemy. No. 3 [Chaps. VII-X]." With an illustrated title page and seven other illustrations. (Jan.), pp. 65-96.

727. Signed illustration to "Pantomimic Distress." *Punch*, 16 (6 Jan.): 3.

728. "Child's Parties: and a Remonstrance Concerning Them." Signed "Spec." With an illustration. *Punch*, 16 (13 Jan.): 13-14.

729. "Child's Parties: and a Remonstrance Concerning Them." Signed "Spec." With an illustration. *Punch*, 16 (27 Jan.): 35-36.

730. "The History of Pendennis. His Fortunes and Misfortunes, His Friends and His Greatest Enemy. No. 4 [Chaps. XI-XIV]." With an illustrated title page and eight other illustrations. (Feb.), pp. 97-128.

731. "England in 1869." With an illustration. *Punch*, 16 (3 Feb.): 51.
("Punch")

732. "Paris Revisited. By An Old Paris Man." Signed "Folkestone Canterbury." With an illustration. *Punch*, 16 (10 Feb.): 55-56. ("Punch")

733. "The Ballad of Bouillabaisse. From the Contributor at Paris." *Punch*, 16 (17 Feb.): 67.

734. "Two or Three Theatres at Paris." [With an illustration by Richard Doyle.] *Punch*, 16 (24 Feb.): 75. ("Punch")

735. "The History of Pendennis. His Fortunes and Misfortunes, His Friends and His Greatest Enemy. No. 5 [Chaps. XV-XVII]." With an illustrated title page and eight other illustrations. (Mar.), pp. 129-60.

736. "On Some Dinners at Paris." Signed "Folkestone Canterbury." [With an illustration by Richard Doyle.] *Punch*, 16 (3 Mar.): 92-93.
("Punch")

737. "The Story of Koompanee Jehan." With an illustration. *Punch*, 16 (17 Mar.): 105-106. ("Punch")

738. "Mr. Brown's Letters to a Young Man About Town. [Introductory Letter.]" With an illustration. *Punch*, 16 (24 Mar.): 115.

739. "Mr. Brown's Letters to a Young Man About Town. On Tailoring—And Toilettes in General." Signed "Brown the Elder." With an illustration. *Punch*, 16 (31 Mar.): 125.

740. "The History of Pendennis. His Fortunes and Misfortunes, His Friends and His Greatest Enemy. No. 6 [Chaps. XVIII-XX]." With an illustrated title page and seven other illustrations. (Apr.), pp. 161-92.

741. "Mr. Brown's Letters to a Young Man About Town. The Influence of Lovely Woman Upon Society." [With an illustration by Richard Doyle.] *Punch*, 16 (7 Apr.): 135-36.

742. "Mr. Brown's Letters to a Young Man About Town. Some More Words About the Ladies." Signed "Brown the Elder." With an illustration. *Punch*, 16 (14 Apr.): 145-46.

743. "Mr. Brown's Letters to a Young Man About Town. On Friendship." Signed "Brown the Elder." With an illustration. *Punch*, 16 (28 Apr.): 165-66.

744. "The History of Pendennis. His Fortunes and Misfortunes, His Friends and His Greatest Enemy. No. 7 [Chaps. XXI-XXIII]." With an illustrated title page and eight other illustrations. (May), pp. 193-224.

745. "Mr. Brown's Letters to a Young Man About Town. On Friendship." Signed "Brown the Elder." *Punch*, 16 (5 May): 184-85.

746. "Mr. Brown's Letters to a Young Man About Town. Brown the Elder Takes Mr. Brown the Younger to a Club." With an illustration. *Punch*, 16 (12 May): 187-88.

747. "Mr. Brown's Letters to a Young Man About Town. Mr. Brown the Elder Takes Mr. Brown the Younger to a Club." *Punch*, 16 (19 May): 197-98.

748. "Mr. Brown's Letters to a Young Man About Town. Mr. Brown the Elder Takes Mr. Brown the Younger to a Club." With an illustration. *Punch*, 16 (26 May): 207-208.

749. "The History of Pendennis. His Fortunes and Misfortunes, His Friends and His Greatest Enemy. No. 8 [Chaps. XXIV-XXVI]." With an illustrated title page and seven other illustrations. (June), pp. 225-56.

750. "Mr. Brown's Letters to a Young Man About Town. A Word About Balls in Season." Signed "Brown the Elder." *Punch*, 16 (9 June): 229-30.

751. "Mr. Brown's Letters to a Young Man About Town. A Word About Dinners." Signed "Brown the Elder." With an illustration. *Punch*, 16 (16 June): 239-40.

752. "Mr. Brown's Letters to a Young Man About Town. On Some Old Customs of the Dinner-Table." Signed "Brown the Elder." With an illustration. *Punch*, 16 (23 June): 249-50.

753. "The History of Pendennis. His Fortunes and Misfortunes, His Friends and His Greatest Enemy. No. 9 [Chaps. XXVII-XXIX]." With an illustrated title page and seven other illustrations. (July), pp. 257-88.

754. "Mr. Brown's Letters to a Young Man About Town. Great and Little Dinners." With an illustration. *Punch*, 17 (7 July): 1-2.

755. "Mr. Brown's Letters to a Young Man About Town. On Love, Marriage, Men and Women." Signed "Brown the Elder." With an illustration. *Punch*, 17 (14 July): 13-14.

756. "Mr. Brown's Letters to a Young Man About Town. On Love, Marriage, Men and Women." With an illustration. *Punch*, 17 (21 July): 23.

757. "The History of Pendennis. His Fortunes and Misfortunes, His Friends and His Greatest Enemy. No. 10 [Chaps. XXX-XXXII]." With an illustrated title page and seven other illustrations. (Aug.), pp. 289-320.

758. "Mr. Brown's Letters to a Young Man About Town. On Love, Marriage, Men and Women." Signed "Brown the Elder." With an illustration. *Punch*, 17 (4 Aug.): 43.

759. "Mr. Brown's Letters to a Young Man About Town. Out Of Town." Signed "Brown the Elder." With an illustration. *Punch*, 17 (11 Aug.): 53.

760. "Mr. Brown's Letters to a Young Man About Town. Out Of Town." Signed "Brown the Elder." With an illustration. *Punch*, 17 (18 Aug.): 66, 69.

761. "News from the Seat of War." With an illustration. *Punch*, 17 (25 Aug.): 73.   ("Punch")

762. "The History of Pendennis. His Fortunes and Misfortunes, His Friends and His Greatest Enemy. No. 11 [Chaps. XXXIII-

XXXVI]." With an illustrated title page and nine other illustrations. (Sept.), pp. 321-52.

763. "What Mr. Jones Saw at Paris." *Punch*, 17 (8 Sept.): 100-101.
("Punch")

764. "Murder of Mr. Cockrobin." With an illustration. *Punch*, 17 (22 Sept.): 119-20.
("Punch")

765. "The Proper Time for Public Executions." *Punch*, 17 (1 Dec.): 214.
("Punch")

766. "Extract from the Letter of a Gentleman in the Service of the Emperor Soulouque." *Punch*, 17 (1 Dec.): 219.
("Punch")

767. Signed illustration to "The Guards and The Line." *Punch*, 17 (22 Dec.): 243.

768. "The Three Sailors." In Samuel Bevan. *Sand and Canvas: A Narrative of Adventures in Egypt* (London: Charles Gilpin, 1849), pp. 340-42.

769. "An Interesting Event. By Mr. Titmarsh." In *The Keepsake*, ed. The Countess of Blessington (London: David Bogue, 1849), pp. 207-15.

1850

770. "The History of Pendennis. His Fortunes and Misfortunes, His Friends and His Greatest Enemy. No. 12 [Chaps. XXXVII-XXXIX]." With an illustrated title page, six other illustrations, and an additional illustrated title page for Volume 1. (Jan.), pp. 353-84.

771. "The Dignity of Literature. To the Editor of the *Morning Chronicle*." *The Morning Chronicle*, 12 Jan., p. 4.
("Chronicle")

772. "Hobson's Choice." With an illustration. *Punch*, 18 (12 Jan.): 11-12.
("Punch")

773. "Hobson's Choice; or, The Perplexities of a Gentleman in Search of a Servant." With two illustrations. *Punch*, 18 (19 Jan.): 21-22.
("Punch")

774. Signed illustration to "The New House of Commons." *Punch*, 18 (19 Jan.): 29.

775. "Hobson's Choice, or The Perplexities of a Gentleman in Search of a Servant." [With an illustration by Richard Doyle.] *Punch*, 18 (26 Jan.): 32-33.　　　　　　　　　　　　　　　　　　　　("Punch")

776. "The History of Pendennis. His Fortunes and Misfortunes, His Friends and His Greatest Enemy. No. 13 [Chaps. I-III]." With an illustrated title page and eight other illustrations. (Feb.), pp. 1-32.

777. "Thoughts on a New Comedy. Being a Letter from Mr. J—s Plush to a Friend." *Punch*, 18 (2 Feb.): 49-50.　　　　　　　　　　　("Punch")

778. "The Ballad of Eliza Davis." Signed "X." With an illustration. *Punch*, 18 (9 Feb.): 53.　　　　　　　　　　　　　　　　　　　　(*Miscellanies*)

779. "Mr. Punch on Church and State Education." *Punch*, 18 (16 Feb.): 61-62.　　　　　　　　　　　　　　　　　　　　　　　　　("Punch")

780. "The Lamentable Ballad of the Foundling of Shoreditch." Signed "X." With an illustration. *Punch*, 18 (23 Feb.): 73.　　　(*Miscellanies*)

781. "The History of Pendennis. His Fortunes and Misfortunes, His Friends and His Greatest Enemy. No. 14 [Chaps. IV-VI]." With an illustrated title page and eight other illustrations. (Mar.), pp. 33-64.

782. "Waiting at the Station." *Punch*, 18 (9 Mar.): 92-93.　　("Punch")

783. "Mr. Finigan's Lament." [With an illustration probably not by Thackeray.] *Punch*, 18 (23 Mar.): 113.　　　　　　　　　　("Punch")

784. "The History of Pendennis. His Fortunes and Misfortunes, His Friends and His Greatest Enemy. No. 15 [Chaps. VII-IX]." With an illustrated title page and eight other illustrations. (Apr.), pp. 65-96.

785. "The Sights of London." Signed "Goliah Muff." With an illustration. *Punch*, 18 (6 Apr.): 132.　　　　　　　　　　　　　　　("Punch")

786. Signed illustration to "The Bachelors' League." *Punch*, 18 (6 Apr.): 138.

787. "Capers and Anchovies. To the Editor of the *Morning Chronicle*." *The Morning Chronicle*, 12 Apr., p. 5.　　　　　　　　　　　("Chronicle")

788. "The Smoke Nuisance." [With an illustration by Richard Doyle.] *Punch*, 18 (13 Apr.): 141.　　　　　　　　　　　　　　　　("Punch")

789. "The Proser. Essays and Discourses by Dr. Solomon Pacifico. I. On A Lady in an Opera-Box." With an illustration. *Punch*, 18 (20 Apr.): 151-52.

790. [Apparently signed illustration to "Admiralty *v.* Assistant-Surgeons. To Colonel Sibthorp." *Punch*, 18 (20 Apr.): 157.]

791. "The History of Pendennis. His Fortunes and Misfortunes, His Friends and His Greatest Enemy. No. 16 [Chaps. X-XIII]." With an illustrated title page and eight other illustrations. (May), pp. 97-128.

792. "The Proser. Essays and Discourses by Dr. Solomon Pacifico. II.— On the Pleasures of Being a Fogy." With an illustration. *Punch*, 18 (4 May): 173.

793. "Lines on a Late Hospicious Ewent. By a Gentleman of the Footguards (Blue)." *Punch*, 18 (11 May): 189.   ("Punch")

794. "The Proser. Essays and Discourses by Dr. Solomon Pacifico. III.— On The Benefits of Being a Fogy." *Punch*, 18 (18 May): 197-98.

795. ["The Wofle New Ballad of Jane Roney and Mary Brown." *Punch*, 18 (25 May): 209.]   (Spielmann, p. 335)

796. "The History of Pendennis. His Fortunes and Misfortunes, His Friends and His Greatest Enemy. No. 17 [Chaps. XIV-XVI]." With an illustrated title page and seven other illustrations. (June), pp. 129-60.

797. "The Proser. Essays and Discourses by Dr. Solomon Pacifico. IV.— On a Good-looking Young Lady." With an illustration. *Punch*, 18 (8 June): 223-24.

798. "The Proser. Essays and Discourses by Dr. Solomon Pacifico. V.— On an Interesting French Exile." *Punch*, 18 (15 June): 234-35.

799. "The Proser. Essays and Discourses by Dr. Solomon Pacifico. VI.— On an American Traveller." *Punch*, 19 (29 June): 7-8.

800. "The History of Pendennis. His Fortunes and Misfortunes, His Friends and His Greatest Enemy. No. 18 [Chaps. XVII-XIX]." With an illustrated title page and eight other illustrations. (July), pp. 161-92.

801. "Mr. Seesaw's Conduct in Parliament during the Late Debates." *Punch*, 19 (6 July): 13.   ("Punch")

802. "A Prospect of Hampton Court." *Punch*, 19 (31 July): 4-5. [Extra number.] ("Punch")

803. "The History of Pendennis. His Fortunes and Misfortunes, His Friends and His Greatest Enemy. No. 19 [Chaps. XX-XXII]." With an illustrated title page and seven other illustrations. (Aug.), pp. 193-224.

804. ["Mr. Molony's Account of the Ball Given to the Nepaulese Ambassador by the Peninsular and Oriental Company." *Punch*, 19 (3 Aug.): 53.] ("Punch")

805. "The Proser. Essays and Discourses by Dr. Solomon Pacifico. VII.—On the Press and the Public." With an illustration. *Punch*, 19 (3 Aug.): 59.

806. Signed illustration to "Generosity to Poor Soldiers." *Punch*, 19 (10 Aug.): 62.

807. "Four Equerries and Three Chaplains." *Punch*, 19 (10 Aug.): 67. ("Punch")

808. "Damages, Two Hundred Pounds." *Punch*, 19 (24 Aug.): 88. ("Punch")

809. "The Lion Huntress of Belgravia. Being Lady Nimrod's Journal of the past Season." [With an illustration probably not by Thackeray.] *Punch*, 19 (24 Aug.): 89-90. ("Punch")

810. "The Lion Huntress of Belgravia. Being Lady Nimrod's Journal of the past Season." With an illustration. *Punch*, 19 (31 Aug.): 91. ("Punch")

811. "The History of Pendennis. His Fortunes and Misfortunes, His Friends and His Greatest Enemy. No. 20 [Chaps. XXIII-XXV]." With an illustrated title page and seven other illustrations. (Sept.), pp. 225-56.

812. "The Lion Huntress of Belgravia. Being Lady Nimrod's Journal of the past Season." *Punch*, 19 (21 Sept.): 123-24. ("Punch")

813. "The Real State of the Case." With an illustration. *Punch*, 19 (28 Sept.): 133. ("Punch")

814. "The History of Pendennis. His Fortunes and Misfortunes, His Friends and His Greatest Enemy. No. 21 [Chaps. XXVI-XXVIII]." With an illustrated title page and eight other illustrations. (Oct.), pp. 257-88.

815. "Murray or Mac Hale." With a signed illustration. *Punch*, 19 (12 Oct.): 155. ("Punch")

816. "Melancholy Musings." *Punch*, 19 (19 Oct.): 170. ("Punch")

817. "The Country in Alarm." Signed "H. Muff." *Punch*, 19 (19 Oct.): 172. ("Punch")

818. "A Retired Neighbourhood." [A drawing, with letterpress.] *Punch*, 19 (26 Oct.): 174. ("Punch")

819. "The Church on the Continent." *Punch*, 19 (26 Oct.): 176. ("Punch")

820. "Pontifical News." *Punch*, 19 (26 Oct.): 182. ("Punch")

821. "The History of Pendennis. His Fortunes and Misfortunes, His Friends and His Greatest Enemy. No. 22 [Chaps. XXIX-XXXII]." With an illustrated title page and eight other illustrations. (Nov.), pp. 289-320.

822. "A Dream of Whitefriars." With two illustrations. *Punch*, 19 (2 Nov.): 184-85. ("Punch")

823. "Fragments from the History of Cashmere. By the Arabian Historian Karagooz. Chap. 222." With an illustration. *Punch*, 19 (23 Nov.): 221. ("Punch")

824. "Mr. Punch's Appeal to an Eminent Appealer." *Punch*, 19 (30 Nov.): 223-24. ("Punch")

825. "The History of Pendennis. His Fortunes and Misfortunes, His Friends and His Greatest Enemy. Nos. 23-24 [Chaps. XXXIII-XXXVII]." With an illustrated title page, ten other illustrations, and an additional illustrated title page for Volume 2. (Dec.), pp. 321-72.

826. "Domestic Scenes—Served with a Writ." With a signed illustration. *Punch*, 19 (14 Dec.): 243. ("Punch")

827. Signed illustration to "Police Regulations for the Publication of Punch's Almanack." *Punch*, 19 (21 Dec.): 254.

828. "Mr. Punch's Address to the Great City of Castlebar." With a signed illustration. *Punch*, 19 (28 Dec.): 263. ("Punch")

829. Preface and short notices to the twenty engravings in Louis Marvy, *Sketches After English Landscape Painters* (London: David Bogue, [1850]).

1851

830. "The Yankee Volunteers." *Punch*, 20 (4 Jan.): 2. ("Punch")

831. ["The Excitement in Belgravia. I. Mr. Butcher and Master Butcher-Boy." [A signed drawing, with letterpress.] *Punch*, 20 (4 Jan.): 8.]
(Spielmann, p. 336)

832. Signed illustration to "Punch's Sermons to Tradesmen. To the Baker." *Punch*, 20 (11 Jan.): 13.

833. "Contract for Muffins." *Punch*, 20 (18 Jan.): 21. ("Punch")

834. "Why Can't They Leave Us Alone in the Holydays?" Signed "Under Petty." *Punch*, 20 (18 Jan.): 23. ("Punch")

835. "Potage à la Cardinal." *Punch*, 20 (18 Jan.): 28. ("Punch")

836. "Religious Persecution." *Punch*, 20 (18 Jan.): 30. ("Punch")

837. "Limerick Butter." *Punch*, 20 (18 Jan.): 30. ("Punch")

838. "Clerical Joke." *Punch*, 20 (18 Jan.): 30. ("Punch")

839. ["The Excitement in Belgravia. Jeames and the Butler." (A drawing, with letterpress.) *Punch*, 20 (25 Jan.): 38.] (Spielmann, p. 336)

840. "A Case of Conscience." *Punch*, 20 (25 Jan.): 38. ("Punch")

841. "A Police Case (In the manner of Mr. L. H.)." *Punch*, 20 (1 Feb.): 44. ("Punch")

842. "Viscount Whiggington's Recal from the Government of Barataria." *Punch*, 20 (1 Feb.): 52. ("Punch")

843. ["No News from Paris. By a Cynical Correspondent." With an illustration. *Punch*, 20 (8 Feb.): 53.] ("Punch")

844. "From the Diario Oltramano." *Punch*, 20 (15 Feb.): 64. ("Punch")

845. "A Plan for a Prize Novel. In a Letter from the eminent Dramatist Brown to the eminent Novelist Snooks." *Punch*, 20 (22 Feb.): 75. ("Punch")

846. "Hurrah for Austria!" *Punch*, 20 (1 Mar.): 86. ("Punch")

847. "A Delicate Case." Signed "Robert Muff." *Punch*, 20 (1 Mar.): 89. ("Punch")

848. "From The Own Correspondent of the Moniteur des Boulevards." Signed "Gobemouche." With an illustration. *Punch*, 20 (8 Mar.): 93. ("Punch")

849. "A Woeful New Ballad of the Protestant Conspiracy to take the Pope's Life. By a Gentleman who has been on the Spot." *Punch*, 20 (15 Mar.): 113. ("Punch")

850. "John Bull Beaten." With an illustration. *Punch*, 20 (22 Mar.): 115-16. ("Punch")

851. "No Business of Ours." Signed "An Oppressed Hindu." With a signed illustration. *Punch*, 20 (29 Mar.): 125-26. ("Punch")

852. "If Not: Why Not?" Signed "Hibernis Hibernior." With an illustration. *Punch*, 20 (5 Apr.): 135. ("Punch")

853. "The French Conspiration." Signed "Gobemouche." *Punch*, 20 (12 Apr.): 146-47. ("Punch")

854. "A Strange Man Just Discovered in Germany." With an illustration. *Punch*, 20 (19 Apr.): 155. ("Punch")

855. "World's Fair Offer." *Punch*, 20 (19 Apr.): 157. ("Punch")

856. "No Exhibition Rabble." *Punch*, 20 (19 Apr.): 157. ("Punch")

857. "To Families Quitting Pimlico." *Punch*, 20 (19 Apr.): 157. ("Punch")

858. "Mr. Molony's Account of the Crystal Palace." *Punch*, 20 (26 Apr.): 171. ("Punch")

859. "May Day Ode." *The Times*, 30 April, p. 5.

860. Signed illustration to "The Original Agapemone in Danger." *Punch*, 20 (3 May): 184.

861. "What I Remarked at the Exhibition." *Punch*, 20 (10 May): 189. ("Punch")

862. "M. Gobemouche's Authentic Account of the Grand Exhibition." Signed "Gobemouche." *Punch*, 20 (10 May): 198. ("Punch")

863. "Festivities at the Middle Temple." *Punch*, 20 (17 May): 200. ("Punch")

864. "The Charles the Second Ball." [With an illustration by John Tenniel.] *Punch*, 20 (24 May): 221. ("Punch")

865. Signed illustration to "Odalisques in the West." *Punch*, 20 (21 June): 255.

866. "Why did the 'America' Beat Us?" *Punch*, 21 (13 Sept.): 118. ("Punch")

867. "Annexation." *Punch*, 21 (13 Sept.): 118. ("Punch")

868. "A Case of Ingratitude." *Punch*, 21 (13 Sept.): 122-23. ("Punch")

869. "A Challenge from Bell's Life." *Punch*, 21 (20 Sept.): 134. ("Punch")

870. "Lines (Not Quite New) Written in a Copy of The Discourses of The Miraculous Doctor." *Punch*, 21 (20 Sept.): 134.   ("Punch")

871. "The Miraculous Cabbage." *Punch*, 21 (20 Sept.): 134. ("Punch")

872. "The Cabbage Rose, Tamisier." *Punch*, 21 (20 Sept.): 135. ("Punch")

873. "A Bid for the New Austrian Loan." *Punch*, 21 (20 Sept.): 136.
                                                                ("Punch")

874. "Palmer's Legs." With a signed illustration. *Punch*, 21 (27 Sept.): 137.   ("Punch")

875. "Panorama of the Inglese—An Inglese Family." *Punch*, 21 (27 Sept.): 138.   ("Punch")

876. "An Ingleez Family." With an illustration. *Punch*, 21 (4 Oct.): 147-48.   ("Punch")

877. "The Knight of Garron Tower." *Punch*, 21 (11 NOct.): 157-58.
                                                                ("Punch")

878. "Poor Puggy." Signed "Swellmore." With an illustration. *Punch*, 21 (18 Oct.): 167.   ("Punch")

879. "Portraits from the Late Exhibition." With three illustrations. *Punch*, 21 (1 Nov.): 190-91.   ("Punch")

880. "County Court Poetry." *Punch*, 21 (8 Nov.): 199.   ("Punch")

881. "Beat It If You Can." *Punch*, 21 (8 Nov.): 208.   ("Punch")

882. "Mr. Molony on the Position of the Bar and Attorneys." Signed "Thaddeus Molony." With an illustration. *Punch*, 21 (15 Nov.): 212.
                                                                ("Punch")

883. Signed illustration to "Fagots for Freemasons." *Punch*, 21 (22 Nov.): 221.

884. "The Last Irish Grievance." [With an illustration by H. R. Howard.] *Punch*, 21 (22 Nov.): 223.   ("Punch")

885. "Voltigeur. By W. M. Thackeray, Esq." In *The Keepsake*, ed. Miss Power (London: David Bogue, 1851), pp. 238-50.

1853

886. ["Mr. Thackeray in the United States. John Small to the Editor of *Fraser's Magazine.*" *Fraser's Magazine*, 47 (Jan.) 100-103.]

887. "Charity and Humour." *Harper's Magazine*, 7 (June): 82-88.

888. Signed illustration to "The Age of Compliments." *Punch*, 25 (1 Oct.): 138.

889. "The Organ Boy's Appeal." *Punch*, 25 (1 Oct.): 141.   ("Punch")

890. "The Newcomes. Memoirs of a Most Respectable Family. No. 1 [Chaps. I-III]." [With an illustrated title page and ten other illustrations by Richard Doyle.] (Oct.), pp. 1-32. (Also in *Harper's Magazine*, 7 [Nov.]: 815-30.)

891. Signed illustration to "Manners and Customs." *Punch*, 25 (8 Oct.): 146.

892. Signed illustration to "Signs Made Symbols." *Punch*, 25 (8 Oct.): 148.

893. "The Newcomes. Memoirs of a Most Respectable Family. No. 2 [Chaps. IV-VI]." [With an illustrated title page and nine other illustrations by Richard Doyle.] (Nov.), pp. 33-64. (Also in *Harper's Magazine*, 8 [Dec.]: 104-18.)

894. "Sorrows of Werther." Signed "W. M. Thackeray." *The Southern Literary Messenger*, 19 (Nov.): 709.

895. "Mr. Washington. To the Editor of The Times." *The Times*, 23 Nov., p. 9.

896. "The Newcomes. Memoirs of a Most Respectable Family. No. 3 [Chaps. VII-IX]." [With an illustrated title page and seven other illustrations by Richard Doyle.] (Dec.), pp. 65-96. (Also in *Harper's Magazine*, 8 [Jan. 1854]: 178-94.)

897. Signed illustration to "A Trumpet with a Cold." *Punch*, 25 (31 Dec.): 267.

898. "Preface," *Mr. Brown's Letters to a Young Man About Town; With The Proser, and Other Papers* (New York: D. Appleton & Co., 1853), pp. ix-xiii.

899. "The Pen and the Album. By W. M. Thackeray." In *The Keepsake*, ed. Miss Power (London: David Bogue, 1853), pp. 48-50.

1854

900. "The Newcomes. Memoirs of a Most Respectable Family. No. 4 [Chaps. X-XII]." [With an illustrated title page and nine other illustrations by Richard Doyle.] (Jan.), pp. 97-128. (Also in *Harper's Magazine*, 8 [Feb.]: 351-65.)

901. "The Newcomes. Memoirs of a Most Respectable Family. No. 5 [Chaps. XIII-XVI]." [With an illustrated title page and nine other illustrations by Richard Doyle.] (Feb.), pp. 129-60. (Also in *Harper's Magazine*, 8 [Apr.]: 637-54.)

902. "The Newcomes. Memoirs of a Most Respectable Family. No. 6 [Chaps. XVII-XX]." [With an illustrated title page and eleven other illustrations by Richard Doyle.] (Mar.), pp. 161-92. (Also in *Harper's Magazine*, 8 [May]: 780-96.)

903. "The Newcomes. Memoirs of a Most Respectable Family. No. 7 [Chaps. XXI-XXIII]." [With an illustrated title page and seven other illustrations by Richard Doyle.] (Apr.), pp. 193-224. (Also in *Harper's Magazine*, 9 [June]: 57-73.)

904. "The Newcomes. Memoirs of a Most Respectable Family. No. 8 [Chaps. XXIV-XXVI]." [With an illustrated title page and seven other illustrations by Richard Doyle.] (May), pp. 225-56. (Also in *Harper's Magazine*, 9 [July]: 201-18.)

905. "The Newcomes. Memoirs of a Most Respectable Family. No. 9 [Chaps. XXVII-XXIX]." [With an illustrated title page and four other illustrations by Richard Doyle.] (June), pp. 257-88. (Also in *Harper's Magazine*, 9 [Aug.]: 348-66.)

906. "Important from the Seat of War! Letters from the East by Our Own Bashi-Bozouk." With a signed illustration. *Punch*, 26 (24 June): 257-58.

907. "The Newcomes. Memoirs of a Most Respectable Family. No. 10 [Chaps. XXX-XXXII]." [With an illustrated title page and eight other illustrations by Richard Doyle.] (July), pp. 289-320. (Also in *Harper's Magazine*, 9 [Sept.]: 492-509.)

908. "Important from the Seat of War! Letters from the East by Our Own Bashi-Bozouk." With an illustration. *Punch*, 26 (1 July): 267-68.

909. "Important from the Seat of War! Letters from the East by Our Own Bashi-Bozouk." *Punch*, 27 (8 July): 1-2.

910. "Important from the Seat of War! Letters from the East by Our Own Bashi-Bozouk." With an illustration. *Punch*, 27 (15 July): 11-12.

911. "Important from the Seat of War! Journal of the Siege of Silistria. By Our Own Bashi-Bozouk." With a signed illustration. *Punch*, 27 (22 July): 21-22.

912. "Important from the Seat of War! Journal of the Siege of Silistria. By Our Own Bashi-Bozouk." With two signed illustrations. *Punch*, 27 (29 July): 31-32.

913. "The Newcomes. Memoirs of a Most Respectable Family. No. 11 [Chaps. XXXIII-XXXV]." [With an illustrated title page and five other illustrations by Richard Doyle.] (Aug.), pp. 321-52. (Also in *Harper's Magazine*, 9 [Oct.]: 618-34.)

914. "Important from the Seat of War! Journal of the Siege of Silistria. By our own Bashi-Bozouk." With an illustration. *Punch*, 27 (5 Aug.): 41.

915. "The Newcomes. Memoirs of a Most Respectable Family. No. 12 [Chaps. XXXVI-XXXVIII]." [With an illustrated title page, four other illustrations, and an additional illustrated title page for Volume 1 by Richard Doyle.] (Sept.), pp. 353-80. (Also in *Harper's Magazine*, 9 [Nov.]: 782-96.)

916. "Mr. Punch to an Eminent Personage." With two illustrations. *Punch*, 27 (16 Sept.): 110-11.   ("Punch")

917. "A Second Letter to an Eminent Personage." With a signed illustration. *Punch*, 27 (23 Sept.): 113-14.   ("Punch")

918. "The Newcomes. Memoirs of a Most Respectable Family. No. 13 [Chaps. I-III]." [With an illustrated title page and seven other illustrations by Richard Doyle.] (Oct.), pp. 1-32. (Also in *Harper's Magazine*, 10 [Dec.]: 61-78.)

919. "The Newcomes. Memoirs of a Most Respectable Family. No. 14 [Chaps. IV-VI]." [With an illustrated title page and seven other illustrations by Richard Doyle.] (Nov.), pp. 33-64. (Also in *Harper's Magazine*, 10 [Jan. 1855]: 222-39.)

920. "The Newcomes. Memoirs of a Most Respectable Family. No. 15 [Chaps. VII-IX]." [With an illustrated title page and seven other

illustrations by Richard Doyle.] (Dec.), pp. 65-96. (Also in *Harper's Magazine*, 10 [Feb.]: 353-71.)

921. "Pictures of Life and Character. By John Leech." *The Quarterly Review*, 96 (Dec.): 75-86.

922. "Lucy's Birthday. By W. M. Thackeray." In *The Keepsake*, ed. Miss Power (London: David Bogue, 1854), p. 18.

1855

923. "The Newcomes. Memoirs of a Most Respectable Family. No. 16 [Chaps. X-XIII]." [With an illustrated title page and seven other illustrations by Richard Doyle.] (Jan.), pp. 97-128. (Also in *Harper's Magazine*, 10 [Mar.]: 511-27.)

924. "The Newcomes. Memoirs of a Most Respectable Family. No. 17 [Chaps. XIV-XVI]." [With an illustrated title page and five other illustrations by Richard Doyle.] (Feb.), pp. 129-60. (Also in *Harper's Magazine*, 10 [Apr.]: 653-70.)

925. "The Newcomes. Memoirs of a Most Respectable Family. No. 18 [Chaps. XVII-XIX]." [With an illustrated title page and seven other illustrations by Richard Doyle.] (Mar.), pp. 161-92. (Also in *Harper's Magazine*, 10 [May]: 799-816.)

926. "The Newcomes. Memoirs of a Most Respectable Family. No. 19 [Chaps. XX-XXIII]." [With an illustrated title page and six other illustrations by Richard Doyle.] (Apr.), pp. 193-224. (Also in *Harper's Magazine*, 11 [June]: 47-64.)

927. "The Newcomes. Memoirs of a Most Respectable Family. No. 20 [Chaps. XXIV-XXVII]." [With an illustrated title page and five other illustrations by Richard Doyle.] (May), pp. 225-56. (Also in *Harper's Magazine*, 11 [July]: 205-21.)

928. "The Newcomes. Memoirs of a Most Respectable Family. No. 21 [Chaps. XXVIII-XXXI]." [With an illustrated title page and seven other illustrations by Richard Doyle.] (June), pp. 257-88. (Also in *Harper's Magazine*, 11 [Aug.]: 335-52.)

929. "The Newcomes. Memoirs of a Most Respectable Family. No. 22 [Chaps. XXXII-XXXV]." [With an illustrated title page and six other illustrations by Richard Doyle.] (July), pp. 289-320. (Also in *Harper's Magazine*, 11 [Sept.]: 479-95.)

930. "The Newcomes. Memoirs of a Most Respectable Family. No. 23-24 [Chaps. XXXVI-XLII]." [With an illustrated title page, ten other illustrations, and an additional illustrated title page for Volume 2 by Richard Doyle.] (Aug.), pp. 321-75. (Also in *Harper's Magazine*, 11 [Oct.]: 622-49.)

931. [Reminiscences of Weimar and Goethe. A letter, 28 April.] In George Henry Lewes, *The Life and Works of Goethe*, 2 vols. (London: David Nutt, 1855), 2: 442-46.

1856

932. ["The Idler." Signed "Essel." *The Idler*, 1 (March): 172-73.]
(*Works*, 7: 204-06)

1857

933. "To the Electors of the City of Oxford. 9 July 1857." [A circular.]

934. "To the Chairmen and Members of the Local Committees. 15 July 1857." [A circular.]

935. "The Sabbath Question. To the Electors of the City of Oxford. 18 July 1857." [A circular.]

936. "The Virginians. A Tale of the Last Century. No. 1 [Chaps. I-IV]." With an illustrated title page and eight other illustrations. (Nov.), pp. 1-32. (Also in *Harper's Magazine*, 16 [Dec.]: 92-108.)

937. "The Virginians. A Tale of the Last Century. No. 2 [Chaps. V-VIII]." With an illustrated title page and five other illustrations. (Dec.), pp. 33-64. (Also in *Harper's Magazine*, 16 [Jan. 1855]: 240-57.)

1858

938. "The Virginians. A Tale of the Last Century. No. 3 [Chaps. IX-XII]." With an illustrated title page and eight other illustrations. (Jan.), pp. 65-96. (Also in *Harper's Magazine*, 16 [Feb.]: 381-98.)

939. "The Virginians. A Tale of the Last Century. No. 4 [Chaps. XIII-XVI]." With an illustrated title page and eight other illustrations. (Feb.), pp. 97-128. (Also in *Harper's Magazine*, 16 [Mar.]: 525-41.)

940. "The Virginians. A Tale of the Last Century. No. 5 [Chaps. XVII-XX]." With an illustrated title page and seven other illustrations. (Mar.), pp. 129-60. (Also in *Harper's Magazine*, 16 [Apr.]: 670-87.)

941. "The Virginians. A Tale of the Last Century. No. 6 [Chaps. XXI-XXIV]." With an illustrated title page and five other illustrations. (Apr.), pp. 161-92. (Also in *Harper's Magazine*, 16 [May]: 813-30.)

942. "The Virginians. A Tale of the Last Century. No. 7 [Chaps. XXV-XXVIII]." With an illustrated title page and six other illustrations. (May), pp. 193-224. (Also in *Harper's Magazine*, 17 [June]: 95-112.)

943. "The Virginians. A Tale of the Last Century. No. 8 [Chaps. XXIX-XXXII." With an illustrated title page and six other illustrations. (June), pp. 225-56. (Also in *Harper's Magazine*, 17 [July]: 239-56.)

944. "The Virginians. A Tale of the Last Century. No. 9 [Chaps. XXXIII-XXXVI]." With an illustrated title page and six other illustrations. (July), pp. 257-88. (Also in *Harper's Magazine*, 17 [Aug.]: 384-401.)

945. "The Virginians. A Tale of the Last Century. No. 10 [Chaps. XXXVII-XL]." With an illustrated title page and six other illustrations. (Aug.), pp. 289-320. (Also in *Harper's Magazine*, 17 [Sept.]: 525-42.)

946. "The Virginians. A Tale of the Last Century. No. 11 [Chaps. XLI-XLIV]." With an illustrated title page and five other illustrations. (Sept.), pp. 321-52. (Also in *Harper's Magazine*, 17 [Oct.]: 669-87.)

947. "The Virginians. A Tale of the Last Century. No. 12 [Chaps. XLV-XLVIII]." With an illustrated title page, six other illustrations, and an additional illustrated title page for Volume 1. (Oct.), pp. 353-82. (Also in *Harper's Magazine*, 17 [Nov.]: 813-29.)

948. "The Virginians. A Tale of the Last Century. No. 13 [Chaps. I-IV]." With an illustrated title page and seven other illustrations. (Nov.), pp. 1-32. (Also in *Harper's Magazine*, 18 [Dec.]: 95-113.)

949. "The Virginians. A Tale of the Last Century. No. 14 [Chaps. V-VIII]." With an illustrated title page and five other illustrations. (Dec.), pp. 33-64. (Also in *Harper's Magazine*, 18 [Jan 1859.]: 237-54.)

1859

950. "The Virginians. A Tale of the Last Century. No. 15 [Chaps. IX-XII]." With an illustrated title page and six other illustrations. (Jan.), pp. 65-96. (Also in *Harper's Magazine*, 18 [Feb.]: 381-99.)

951. "The Virginians. A Tale of the Last Century. No. 16 [Chaps. XIII-XV]." With an illustrated title page and five other illustrations. (Feb.), pp. 97-128. (Also in *Harper's Magazine*, 18 [Mar.]: 525-43.)

952. "The Virginians. A Tale of the Last Century. No. 17 [Chaps. XVI-XIX]." With an illustrated title page and six other illustrations. (Mar.), pp. 129-60. (Also in *Harper's Magazine*, 18 [Apr.]: 670-86.)

953. "The Virginians. A Tale of the Last Century. No. 18 [Chaps. XX-XXIII]." With an illustrated title page and six other illustrations. (Apr.), pp. 161-92. (Also in *Harper's Magazine*, 18 [May]: 816-33.)

954. "The Virginians. A Tale of the Last Century. No. 19 [Chaps. XXIV-XXVII]." With an illustrated title page and six other illustrations. (May), pp. 193-224. (Also in *Harper's Magazine*, 19 [June]: 101-18.)

955. "The Virginians. A Tale of the Last Century. No. 20 [Chaps. XXVIII-XXXI]." With an illustrated title page and six other illustrations. (June), pp. 225-56. (Also in *Harper's Magazine*, 19 [July]: 240-55.)

956. "The Virginians. A Tale of the Last Century. No. 21 [Chaps. XXXII-XXXV]." With an illustrated title page and six other illustrations. (July), pp. 257-88. (Also in *Harper's Magazine*, 19 [Aug.]: 381-98.)

957. "The Virginians. A Tale of the Last Century. No. 22 [Chaps. XXXVI-XXXVIII]." With an illustrated title page and three other illustrations. (Aug.), pp. 289-320. (Also in *Harper's Magazine*, 19 [Sept.]: 537-54.)

958. "The Virginians. A Tale of the Last Century. No. 23 [Chaps. XXXIX-XLII]." With an illustrated title page and eight other illustrations. (Sept.), pp. 321-52. (Also in *Harper's Magazine*, 19 [Oct.]: 677-94.)

959. "The Virginians. A Tale of the Last Century. No. 24 [Chaps. XLIII-XLIV]." With an illustrated title page, three other illustrations, and an additional illustrated title page for Volume 2. (Oct.), pp. 353-76. (Also in *Harper's Magazine*, 19 [Nov.]: 818-30.)

960. "To a Contributor." 1 November 1859. [A circular laid into copies of the January 1860 number of *The Cornhill Magazine*.]

1860

961. "Lovel the Widower [Chap. I]." With two illustrations. *The Cornhill Magazine*, 1 (Jan.): 44-60. (Also in *Harper's Magazine*, 20 [Feb.]: 383-92.)

962. "Roundabout Papers.—No. I. On A Lazy Idle Boy." With an illustration. *The Cornhill Magazine*, 1 (Jan.): 124-28.

963. "Nil Nisi Bonum." *The Cornhill Magazine*, 1 (Feb.): 129-34. (Also in *Harper's Magazine*, 20 [Mar.]: 542-45.)

964. "Lovel the Widower [Chap. II]." With two illustrations. *The Cornhill Magazine*, 1 (Feb.): 233-47. (Also in *Harper's Magazine*, 20 [Mar.]: 525-34.)

965. "Lovel the Widower [Chap. III]." With two illustrations. *The Cornhill Magazine*, 1 (Mar.): 330-45. (Also in *Harper's Magazine*, 20 [Apr.]: 680-88.)

966. "Roundabout Papers.—No. II. On Two Children in Black." *The Cornhill Magazine*, 1 (Mar.): 380-84. (Also in *Harper's Magazine*, 20 [Apr.], 670-72.)

967. "Lovel the Widower [Chap. IV]." With two illustrations. *The Cornhill Magazine*, 1 (Apr.): 385-402. (Also in *Harper's Magazine*, 20 [May]: 813-24.)

968. "The Last Sketch." Signed "W. M. T." *The Cornhill Magazine*, 1 (Apr.): 485-87. (Also in *Harper's Magazine*, 20 [May]: 824-25.)

969. "Lovel the Widower [Chap. V]." With two illustrations. *The Cornhill Magazine*, 1 (May): 583-97. (Also in *Harper's Magazine*, 21 [June]: 99-107.)

970. "Roundabout Papers.—No. III. On Ribbons." With an illustration [and another illustration engraved from a photograph]. *The Cornhill Magazine*, 1 (May): 631-40.

971. "Lovel the Widower [Chap. VI]." With two illustrations. *The Cornhill Magazine*, 1 (June): 652-68. (Also in *Harper's Magazine*, 21 [July]: 238-47.)

972. "Roundabout Papers.—No. IV. On Some Late Great Victories." With an illustration. *The Cornhill Magazine*, 1 (June): 755-60.

973. "The Four Georges. Sketches of Manners, Morals, Court and Town Life. I.—George the First." With three illustrations. *The Cornhill Magazine*, 2 (July): 1-20. (Also in *Harper's Magazine*, 21 [Aug.]: 395-405.)

974. "Vanitas Vanitatum." *The Cornhill Magazine,* 2 (July): 59-60.

975. "Roundabout Papers.—No. V. Thorns in the Cushion." With an illustration. *The Cornhill Magazine,* 2 (July): 122-28.

976. "The Four Georges. Sketches of Manners, Morals, Court, and Town Life. II.—George the Second." With three illustrations. *The Cornhill Magazine,* 2 (Aug.): 175-91. (Also in *Harper's Magazine,* 21 [Sept.]: 525-35.)

977. "Roundabout Papers.—No. VI. On Screens in Dining-rooms." With an illustration. *The Cornhill Magazine,* 2 (Aug.): 252-56.

978. "The Four Georges. Sketches of Manners, Morals, Court, and Town Life. III.—George the Third." With four illustrations. *The Cornhill Magazine,* 2 (Sept.): 257-77. (Also in *Harper's Magazine,* 21 [Oct.]: 671-82.)

979. "Roundabout Papers.—No. VII. Tunbridge Toys." With an illustration. *The Cornhill Magazine,* 2 (Sept.): 380-84.

980. "The Four Georges. Sketches of Manners, Morals, Court, and Town Life. IV.—George the Fourth." With two illustrations. *The Cornhill Magazine,* 2 (Oct.): 385-406. (Also in *Harper's Magazine,* 21 [Nov.]: 823-34.)

981. "Roundabout Papers.—No. VIII. De Juventute." With three illustrations. *The Cornhill Magazine,* 2 (Oct.): 500-12.

982. "A Roundabout Journey. Notes of a Week's Holiday. With three illustrations. *The Cornhill Magazine,* 2 (Nov.): 623-40.

983. "Roundabout Papers.—No. IX. On a Joke I Once Heard From The Late Thomas Hood." With two illustrations. *The Cornhill Magazine,* 2 (Dec): 752-60.

1861

984. "The Adventures of Philip on his way through the World; Shewing Who Robbed Him, Who Helped Him, and Who Passed Him By [Chaps. I-III]." With two illustrations [and one by Frederick Walker]. *The Cornhill Magazine,* 3 (Jan.): 1-24. (Also in *Harper's Magazine,* 22 [Feb.]: 381-93.)

985. "Philip [Chaps. IV-V]." With two illustrations [and one by Frederick Walker]. *The Cornhill Magazine,* 3 (Feb.): 166-89. (Also in *Harper's Magazine,* 22 [Mar.]: 529-42.)

986. "Roundabout Papers.—No. X. Round About The Christmas Tree." With an illustration. *The Cornhill Magazine*, 3 (Feb): 250-56.

987. "Philip [Chaps. VI-VII]." With two illustrations [and one by Frederick Walker]. *The Cornhill Magazine*, 3 (Mar.): 270-93. (Also in *Harper's Magazine*, 22 [Apr.]: 669-82.)

988. "Philip [Chaps. VIII-X]." With three illustrations [and one by Frederick Walker]. *The Cornhill Magazine*, 3 (Apr.): 385-408. (Also in *Harper's Magazine*, 22 [May]: 815-27.)

989. "Roundabout Papers.—No. XI. On a Chalk Mark on the Door." With an illustration. *The Cornhill Magazine*, 3 (Apr.): 504-12.

990. "Philip [Chaps. XI-XII]." With two illustrations [and one by Frederick Walker]. *The Cornhill Magazine*, 3 (May): 556-83. (Also in *Harper's Magazine*, 23 [June]: 90-105.)

991. "Roundabout Papers.—No. XII. On Being Found Out." With an illustration. *The Cornhill Magazine*, 3 (May): 636-40. (Also in *Harper's Magazine*, 23 [June]: 112-14.)

992. "Philip [Chaps. XIII-XIV]." With two illustrations [and one by Frederick Walker]. *The Cornhill Magazine*, 3 (June): 641-65. (Also in *Harper's Magazine*, 23 [July]: 233-46.)

993. "Roundabout Papers.—No. XIII. On a Hundred Years Hence." With an illustration. *The Cornhill Magazine*, 3 (June): 755-60.

994. "Philip [Chaps. XV-XVI]." With two illustrations [and one by Frederick Walker]. *The Cornhill Magazine*, 4 (July): 1-24. (Also in *Harper's Magazine*, 23 [Aug.]: 381-94.)

995. "Roundabout Papers.—No. XIV. Small Beer Chronicle." With two illustrations. *The Cornhill Magazine*, 4 (July): 122-28.

996. "Philip [Chaps. XVII-XVIII]." With two illustrations [and one by Frederick Walker]. *The Cornhill Magazine*, 4 (Aug.): 129-52. (Also in *Harper's Magazine*, 23 [Sept.]: 524-37.)

997. "Roundabout Papers.—No. XV. Ogres." With an illustration. *The Cornhill Magazine*, 4 (Aug.): 251-56.

998. "Philip [Chaps. XIX-XX]." With two illustrations [and one by Frederick Walker]. *The Cornhill Magazine*, 4 (Sept.): 257-80. (Also in *Harper's Magazine*, 23 [Oct.]: 689-702.)

999. "Roundabout Papers.—No. XVI. On Two Roundabout Papers Which I Intended To Write." With an illustration. *The Cornhill Magazine*, 4 (Sept.): 377-84.

1000. "Philip [Chaps. XXI-XXII]." With two illustrations [and one by Frederick Walker]. *The Cornhill Magazine*, 4 (Oct.): 385-408. (Also in *Harper's Magazine*, 23 [Nov.]: 819-32.)

1001. "Philip [Chaps. XXIII-XXIV]." With two illustrations [and one by Frederick Walker]. *The Cornhill Magazine*, 4 (Nov.): 513-36. (Also in *Harper's Magazine*, 24 [Dec.]: 90-103.)

1002. "Philip [Chaps. XXV-XXVI]." With two illustrations [and one by Frederick Walker]. *The Cornhill Magazine*, 4 (Dec.): 641-64. (Also in *Harper's Magazine*, 24 [Jan. 1862]: 233-45.)

1003. "Roundabout Papers.—No. XVII. A Mississippi Bubble." With an illustration. *The Cornhill Magazine*, 4 (Dec.): 754-60.

1004. "A Leaf out of a Sketch-Book. By W. M. Thackeray." With two illustrations. *The Victoria Regia: A Volume of Original Contributions in Poetry and Prose*, ed. Adelaide A. Procter (London: Emily Faithfull, 1861), pp. 118-25.

1862

1005. "Philip [Chaps. XXVII-XXVIII]." With two illustrations [and one by Frederick Walker]. *The Cornhill Magazine*, 5 (Jan.): 1-24. (Also in *Harper's Magazine*, 24 [Feb.]: 379-92.)

1006. "Roundabout Papers.—No. XVIII. On Lett's Diary." With an illustration. *The Cornhill Magazine*, 5 (Jan.): 122-28.

1007. "Philip [Chaps. XXIX-XXX]." With two illustrations [and one by Frederick Walker]. *The Cornhill Magazine*, 5 (Feb.): 129-52. (Also in *Harper's Magazine*, 24 [Mar.]: 522-35.)

1008. "Roundabout Papers.—No. XIX. On Half A Loaf. A Letter to Messrs. Broadway, Battery & Co., of New York, Bankers." With an illustration. *The Cornhill Magazine*, 5 (Feb.): 250-56.

1009. "Philip [Chaps. XXXI-XXXII]." With two illustrations [and one by Frederick Walker]. *The Cornhill Magazine*, 5 (Mar.): 257-80. (Also in *Harper's Magazine*, 24 [Apr.]: 684-96.)

1010. [To] Contributors and Correspondents *The Cornhill Magazine.* 25 March 1862. [A circular laid into copies of the April 1862 number]

1011. "Philip [Chaps. XXXIII-XXXIV]." With two illustrations [and one by Frederick Walker]. 5 (Apr.): 385-408. (Also in *Harper's Magazine,* 24 [May]: 823-35.)

1012. "Roundabout Papers.—No. XX. The Notch on the Axe.—A Story *à la Mode.* Part I." With an illustration. *The Cornhill Magazine,* 5 (Apr.): 508-12.

1013. "Philip [Chaps. XXXV-XXXVI]." With two illustrations [and one by Frederick Walker]. *The Cornhill Magazine,* 5 (May): 513-36. (Also in *Harper's Magazine,* 25 [June]: 99-112.)

1014. "Roundabout Papers.—No. XXI. The Notch on the Axe.—A Story *à la Mode.* Part II." With an illustration. *The Cornhill Magazine,* 5 (May): 634-40.

1015. "Philip [Chaps. XXXVII-XXXVIII]." With two illustrations[and one by Frederick Walker]. *The Cornhill Magazine,* 5 (June): 641-64. (Also in *Harper's Magazine,* 25 [July]: 237-49.)

1016. "Roundabout Papers.—No. XXII. The Notch on the Axe.—A Story *à la Mode.* Part III." With an illustration. *The Cornhill Magazine,* 5 (June): 754-60.

1017. "Mr. Leech's Sketches in Oil." *The Times,* 2 June, p. 5.

1018. "Philip [Chaps. XXXIX-XL]." With two illustrations [and one by Frederick Walker]. *The Cornhill Magazine,* 6 (July): 121-44. (Also in *Harper's Magazine,* 25 [Aug.]: 404-16.)

1019. "Philip [Chaps. XLI-XLII]." With two illustrations [and one by Frederick Walker]. *The Cornhill Magazine,* 6 (Aug.): 217-40. (Also in *Harper's Magazine,* 25 [Sept.]: 533-45.)

1020. "Roundabout Papers.—No. XXIII. De Finibus." With an illustration. *The Cornhill Magazine,* 6 (Aug.): 282-88.

1021. "Roundabout Papers.—No. XXIV. On a Peal of Bells." With an illustration. *The Cornhill Magazine,* 6 (Sept.): 425-32.

1022. "Roundabout Papers.—No. XXV. On a Pear Tree." With an illustration. *The Cornhill Magazine,* 6 (Nov.): 715-20.

1023. "Roundabout Papers.—No. XXVI. Dessein's." With an illustration. *The Cornhill Magazine,* 6 (Dec.): 771-79.

1863

1024. "Roundabout Papers.—No. XXVII. On Some Carp at Sans Souci." With an illustration. *The Cornhill Magazine*, 7 (Jan.): 126-31.

1025. "Roundabout Papers.—No. XXVIII. Autour de mon Chapeau." With an illustration. *The Cornhill Magazine*, 7 (Feb.): 260-67.

1026. "On Alexandrines. A Letter to Some Country Cousins." With an illustration. *The Cornhill Magazine*, 7 (Apr.): 546-52.

1027. "Cruikshank's Gallery." *The Times*, 15 May, p. 6.

1028. "On a Medal of George the Fourth." *The Cornhill Magazine*, 8 (Aug.): 250-56.

1029. "'Strange to Say, on Club Paper.'" With an illustration. *The Cornhill Magazine*, 8 (Nov.): 636-40.

1864

1030. "Denis Duval [Chaps. I-III]." [With two illustrations by Frederick Walker.] *The Cornhill Magazine*, 9 (Mar.): 257-91. (Also in *Harper's Magazine*, 28 [Apr.]: 675-92.)

1031. "Denis Duval [Chaps. IV-V]." [With two illustrations by Frederick Walker.] *The Cornhill Magazine*, 9 (Apr.): 385-409. (Also in *Harper's Magazine*, 28 [May]: 815-28.)

1032. "Denis Duval [Chaps. VI-VII]." [With two illustrations by Frederick Walker.] *The Cornhill Magazine*, 9 (May): 513-36. (Also in *Harper's Magazine*, 29 [June]: 213-26.)

1033. "Denis Duval [Chap. VIII]." [With two illustrations by Frederick Walker and a "Note by the Editor."] *The Cornhill Magazine*, 9 (June): 641-65. (Also in *Harper's Magazine*, 29 [July]: 358-71.)

APPENDIX

Possible Thackeray Illustrations

(These are unsigned illustrations accompanying the works of other writers in *Punch*, and reprinted without cited evidence in the Oxford Edition of Thackeray's works.)

1843

A1. Illustration [?] to "A Commission of Inquiry into the State of the Aristocracy." *Punch*, 5 (1 July): 2.

A2. Two illustrations [?] to "Present to the Duke of Wellington. (From Our Own Reporter.)" *Punch*, 5 (14 Oct.): 161-62.

1844

A3. Illustration [?] to "Notice." *Punch*, 6 (20 Jan.): 42.

1845

A4. Illustration [?] to "Punch's Guide to Servants. The Clerk." *Punch*, 9 (12 July): 29.

1846

A5. Illustration [?] to "High Court of Public Opinion." *Punch*, 11 (3 Oct.): 143.

A6. Illustration [?] to "Theatrical Intelligence Extraordinary." *Punch*, 11 (17 Oct.): 166.

A7. Illustration [?] to "Theatrical Astronomy. Sudden Appearance of a Star." *Punch*, 11 (24 Oct.): 175.

A8. Illustration [?] to "Provincial Theatricals." *Punch*, 11 (31 Oct.): 183.

1847

A9. Illustration [?] to "Punch's Songs for the (Thames) Navy." *Punch*, 12 (1 May): 178.

A10. Illustration [?] to "Musical Criticisms." *Punch,* 12 (10 Apr.): 146.

A11. Illustration [?] to "The Bore of the Billet. To Illustrious Quarters." *Punch,* 12 (26 June): 263.

A12. Illustration [?] to "The Sailors' Serenade." *Punch,* 13 (11 Sept.): 91.

A13. Illustration [?] to "The 'Retail Trade' in the House of Commons." *Punch,* 13 (25 Sept.): 111.

A14. Illustration [?] to "Bunn's Prose." *Punch,* 13 (2 Oct.): 124.

A15. Three illustrations [?] to "Punch at the Play." *Punch,* 13 (16 Oct.): 141.

A16. Illustration [?] to "Another New Chapter for 'The Seven Champions of Christendom.'" *Punch,* 13 (30 Oct.): 163.

A17. Illustration [?] to "Baronial Balls." *Punch,* 13 (6 Nov.): 172.

A18. Two illustrations [?] to "Colonial Annuals." *Punch,* 13 (6 Nov.): 180.

A19. Illustration [?] to "Punch at the Play." *Punch,* 13 (13 Nov.): 182.

A20. Illustration [?] to "The Shakspeare Night." *Punch,* 13 (11 Dec.): 221.

A21. Illustration [?] to "England's Weak Points." *Punch,* 13 (11 Dec.): 227.

A22. Illustration [?] to "Our Home Expresses." Punch, 13 (18 Dec.): 233.

A23. Illustration [?] to "The Defences of the Country." *Punch,* 13 (25 Dec.): 250.

1848

A24. Illustration [?] to "The French at Brighton." *Punch,* 14 (29 Jan.): 42.

A25. Illustration [?] to "Something of National Importance." *Punch,* 14 (19 Feb.): 71.

A26. Illustration [?] to "The Mystery Unravelled." *Punch,* 14 (11 Mar.): 99.

A27. Illustration [?] to "The Ragged Revolution: Ragged Letters." *Punch,* 14 (29 Apr.): 176.

A28. Illustration [?] to "The Model Wife." *Punch*, 14 (6 May): 187.

A29. Illustration [?] to "Great Meeting of Petticoat Patriots. British Manufactures!" *Punch*, 14 (6 May): 193.

A30. Illustration [?] to "The Model Gentleman." *Punch*, 14 (27 May): 226.

A31. Illustration [?] to "The Model Lodging-House Keeper." *Punch*, 15 (5 Aug.): 55.

A32. Four illustrations [?] to "The Shell-Jacket and the Army." *Punch*, 15 (5 Aug.): 62-63.

A33. Illustration [?] to "Advertisement. To the Bitten Gentleman." *Punch*, 15 (28 Oct.): 191.

A34. Illustration [?] to "Rogues and Revolutions." *Punch*, 15 (9 Dec.): 245.

A35. Illustration [?] to "The House-keeping Club." *Punch*, 15 (30 Dec.): 273.

1849

A36. Illustration [?] to "Deeper and Deeper Still." *Punch*, 16 (2 June): 226.

A37. Illustration [?] to "Astleian History of the Indian War." *Punch*, 17 (7 July): 10.

A38. Illustration [?] to "The War Congress." *Punch*, 17 (1 Sept.): 85.

A39. Illustration [?] to "Baker Street, A Penal Settlement." *Punch*, 17 (6 Oct.): 141.

1850

A40. Illustration [?] to "'An Appeal to the Aristocracy.'" *Punch*, 18 (16 Feb.): 69.

A41. Illustration [?] to "A Mew from the Cat." *Punch*, 18 (27 Apr.): 163.

A42. Illustration [?] to "A Bit of My Mind. Bit the Sixteenth." *Punch*, 19 (17 Aug.): 71

A43. Illustration [?] to "Hey! for Scotland's Law." Punch, 19 (24 Aug.): 87.

A44. Illustration [?] to "The Hippopotamus in a New Character." *Punch*, 19 (31 Aug.): 92.

A45. Illustration [?] to "To Persons about to Marry. A Card." *Punch*, 19 (14 Sept.): 113.

A46. Illustration [?] to "Early Closing of Glen Tilt." *Punch*, 19 (21 Sept.): 124.

A47. Illustration [?] to "The Parks and the People." *Punch*, 19 (5 Oct.): 144.

A48. Illustration [?] to "Sheriff Carden on 'The Army and Navy.'" *Punch*, 19 (12 Oct.): 154.

A49. Illustration [?] to "Aggression on the Omnibus Roofs." *Punch*, 19 (16 Nov.): 210.

A50. Illustration [?] to "Revivals." *Punch*, 19 (23 Nov.) 213.

A51. Illustration [?] to "Timely Caution." *Punch*, 19 (28 Dec.): 266.

1851

A52. Illustration [?] to "The Sense of Being Married. (Paragraph for a Ladies' Page.)" *Punch*, 20 (11 Jan.): 12.

A53. Illustration [?] to "Ministerial Movements. (From our own Reporter.)" *Punch*, 20 (8 Mar.): 94.

A54. Illustration [?] to "The Wrongs of Pimlico." *Punch*, 20 (19 Apr.): 155.

A55. Illustration [?] to "The Language of Music." *Punch*, 20 (3 May): 175.

A56. Illustration [?] to "Visions in the Crystal." *Punch*, 20 (10 May): 188.

A57. Illustration [?] to "May Day in London, according to Jonathan. (Expressly Made for the 'New York Herald.')" *Punch*, 20 (10 May): 192.

A58. Illustration [?] to "Newdegate on Nunneries. To the Editor of the 'Tablet.'" *Punch*, 20 (24 May): 209.

A59. Illustration [?] to "More Protestant Prejudice." *Punch*, 20 (24 May): 220.

A60. Illustration [?] to "The British Broom Girls." *Punch*, 20 (31 May): 222.

A61. Illustration [?] to "The Bull and the Scarlet Stockings." *Punch*, 20 (14 June): 243.

A62. Illustration [?] to "Mammon and the Bishops." *Punch*, 21 (4 Oct.): 148.

A63. Illustration [?] to "Punch's Notes and Queries." *Punch*, 21 (11 Oct.): 163.

INDEX

References are made to item numbers in the Checklist. Numerals preceded by "A" refer to items in the Appendix. Book reviews appear under the name of the original author.

INDEX OF ILLUSTRATIONS

ENGLISH LITERARY STUDIES MONOGRAPH SERIES

ENGLISH LITERARY STUDIES publishes peer-reviewed monographs (usual length, 45,000-60,000 words) on the literatures written in English. The Series is open to a wide range of scholarly and critical methodologies, and it considers for publication bibliographies, scholarly editions, and historical and critical studies of significant authors, texts, and issues. ELS publishes two to five monographs annually.